Conservation Law in the Countryside

Tolley Publishing Company Limited

Conservation Law in the Countryside

by Michael Gregory OBE LLB, Barrister

Tolley Publishing Company Limited
A UNITED NEWSPAPERS PUBLICATION

ISBN 0 85459 758–1

First published 1994

Published by
Tolley Publishing Company Ltd
Tolley House
2 Addiscombe Road
Croydon
Surrey
CR9 5AF
081–686 9141

Typeset in Great Britain by
Kerrypress Ltd, Luton, Bedfordshire

Printed and bound in Great Britain by
Hobbs the Printers, Southampton

Preface

The love of the public for our wondrous countryside was, for a long time, careless love. In recent times, however, public awareness has been acutely aroused to the ability of modern technology to savage every part of the environment, from the groundwater below the surface to the upper layers of the atmosphere. The individual may feel helpless against the polluter, the vandal, the greedy, the reckless, the noisy, the "litterbug" or the thoughtless, but the power of public opinion is demonstrated by the recent acceleration in the production of environmental legislation from Westminster and Brussels.

The last few years have spawned statutes weighty in import and avoirdupois, though veritable spaghetti junctions of complexity. This book aims to guide the way through these and earlier conservation laws in a manner helpful to the practitioner, and which can also be understood by the many without legal training who are concerned with the protection of the countryside, and who may need to exercise rights of objection. An attempt has been made to make opaque and intricate statutory drafting comprehensible without loss of accuracy. In a book of this size, not every exception, proviso and wrinkle of the law can be examined, but statutory and other references have been freely given to guide the way, and to warn of amending afterthoughts. Alas, Parliament has acquired a confusing habit of amending Acts almost as soon as they are passed. The Environmental Protection Act 1990 was so busy at it, it even amended a section of its own, by one of its schedules, before it was passed!

The chapters ahead cover the sundry environmental designations of land and the authorities with responsibilities in the countryside, in particular the changed set-up brought in by the Environmental Protection Act 1990. The new laws that hefty measure introduced for integrated pollution control, clean air, statutory nuisances, waste regulation and disposal, litter and genetically modified organisms, along with other legislation and the common law, are dealt with in a chapter on dangers and nuisances, ranging from hazardous substances to stubble burning.

Five statutes in 1991 gathered together the reform of the law for the protection and management of waters. The book explains how the creation of the National Rivers Authority, with responsibility in particular for water resources, water quality and fisheries, was revolutionary, and examines the laws for abstraction, pollution, droughts, flood defence and fisheries. The great body of town and country planning laws, underpinning all conservation law, consolidated in four complex Acts of 1990 (already much amended), is outlined, as well as the laws governing environmentally sensitive areas, nitrate sensitive areas, forests, trees, hedgerows, mineral workings, commons and treasure trove.

A chapter on wildlife covers the safeguarding of wild birds, animals, plants, fish and endangered species, including the Protection of Badgers Act 1992, the Deer Act 1991 and the Conservation of Seals Act 1970. Listed buildings, conservation areas, and our rich heritage of ancient monuments and sites of archaeological importance are given a chapter.

The wellbeing of the countryside depends to a crucial extent on those who own, occupy and live in it. A feature of the book is an explanation of the initiatives open to landowners, farmers, communities and groups, for rural conservation, including schemes for farming set-aside and conservation grants, countryside stewardship, farm woodlands, wildlife enhancement, volunteer action and many others.

I am indebted and grateful to the many organisations mentioned in the text who have provided me with information and guidance, especially the Department of the Environment, the Department of National Heritage, the Ministry of Agriculture, Fisheries and Food, the Countryside Commission, the Countryside Council for Wales, English Nature, English Heritage, Cadw, the Forestry Commission, the Rural Development Commission, the Farming and Wildlife Trust, the Country Landowners' Association and the National Farmers' Union. I offer my thanks to the skilful publishers and printers of this book, and to the beloved members of my household, and visiting grandchildren, for keeping patience with me and their sticky fingers off the voluminous papers accumulated for this work cluttering up living space.

Unhappily, the English language does not have a collective pronoun to embrace persons without distinction of sex. To shorten sentences, the convention of using "he", "his" and "him" is adopted to mean "he or she", "his or hers" and "him or her".

Contents

Contents

Table of Statutes

Table of Statutory Instruments

Table of Cases

Chapter 1

Conservation law for a living countryside

The growth of public concern for the protection of the environment in the last few decades has been rapid and infectious. Law lags behind public opinion, but as politicians, our very legislators, have, with the spur of public opinion in their sides, turned to ever brighter shades of green, conservation law has developed apace. It continues to do so in the UK, in Europe and internationally.

The direst environmental problems are global. The depletion of the ozone layer, "global warming" and the preservation of endangered species of fauna and flora, for example, require international solutions. One nation's emissions can be another's pollution. Sulphur dioxide and oxides of nitrogen emitted from chimneys in one country will cause acid rain to poison lakes and rivers a thousand miles away in other countries. The Chernobyl nuclear disaster in April 1986 contaminated sheep as far away from the site in Russia as the UK. Measures binding nations internationally are needed to combat these perils.

1. International laws

A word about the difficult subject of international law is therefore called for. It is difficult not just because international law is esoteric, but also because it is veiled in mists of uncertainty. Unfortunately international law is the weakest of laws and the International Court of Justice a tribunal with scant power to dent the self-interest of nations.

This is not to say it is ineffective or that accords between nations are of no account. As noted in Chapter 2, a treaty ratified by the contracting states creates binding obligations, but, especially on environmental matters, treaties tend to be vague or temporising if they are to get wide ratification—and the basis of liability in international law between nations, or between citizens of one country and the government of another, is acknowledged by jurists to be unclear, even dubious.

The UN Stockholm Declaration on the Human Environment (1972) laid down principles, not edicts, but it put in train initiatives for concerted action to tackle global problems—though the train is slow-moving. The principles were reaffirmed by 105 states at the Nairobi Convention in 1982, and the following year the UN formed the World Commission on Environment and Development. Progress continued to the so-called Earth Summit at Rio de Janeiro in 1992, where treaties were signed on climate change and on biodiversity of species to protect endangered plants and animals. Although Rio gave no impression of urgent action, it did spawn more than words. Programmes were set up for international studies and exchanges of skills, and governments reached for their wallets.

(a) Finance

Money is needed to get over most difficulties in life, and so it is with the environment. At Rio the British Prime Minister committed Britain to increase by £100m its contribution to the Global Environment Facility for programmes on climate change, and he announced further new expenditure of £25m on other projects. The Environmental Protection Act 1990 enables the UK government to do this. It specifically allows financial assistance to be given to the UN Environment Programme; the European Environment Programme; the chemicals programme of the OECD; the joint inter-governmental panel on Climate Change of the UN Environment Programme and the World Meteorological Organisation; the International Union for the Conservation of Nature and Natural Resources; the Convention on International Trade in Endangered Species of Wild Fauna and Flora; the Convention on Wetlands of International Importance Especially as Waterfowl Habitat; the Convention on Long-range Transboundary Air Pollution; the Convention for the Protection of the Ozone Layer; the Convention on the Conservation of Migratory Species of Wild Animals; the Groundwork Foundation and Trusts; the environmental protection technology scheme; and the special grants programme so far as it relates to the protection, improvement or better understanding of the environment of Great Britain (s 153).

Section 156 of the Environmental Protection Act 1990 allows the Secretary of State to make regulations modifying certain provisions of the Act to give effect to European Community obligations, or obligations under any international agreement to which the UK is a party. The provisions concerned are those relating to integrated pollution control, air pollution control, waste, genetically modified organisms and the import, use, supply and storage of injurious substances and waste. Regulations can likewise be made modifying radioactive substances legislation.

2. Europe

The European Community has built up a sizeable body of environmental law. Chapter 2 explains how some is binding directly on member states while some is implemented by member states enacting domestic legislation.

3. The UK

In the UK, major conservation legislation has been enacted in recent years and the Government issued a commitment to environmental protection in a big way in its comprehensive White Paper, *This Common Inheritance* (1990 Cm 1200). The Planning Policy Guide on *The Countryside and the Rural Economy* (DoE PPG7, January 1992) neatly summarised the White Paper's domestic policies for the countryside by stating that they were based on sound stewardship of the heritage and on creating the conditions for a healthy and growing economy by:

(a) encouraging economic activity in rural areas;

(b) conserving and improving the landscape, and encouraging opportunities for recreation; and

(c) conserving the diversity of wildlife, particularly by protecting and enhancing habitats (para 1.1).

Some of the recent legislation gives effect, among its many other provisions, to treaty obligations and Community law, and the Food and Environment Protection Act 1985, s 16 declares:

"This Part of this Act shall have effect with a view to the continuous development of means—

(i) to protect the health of human beings, creatures and plants;

(ii) to safeguard the environment; and

(iii) to secure safe, efficient and humane methods of controlling pests . . .".

It is something of a let-down to find that this desirable consummation shall be by way of regulations to be made by Ministers in their own good time, but important regulations have been made under the Act, and it was not so long ago when such ideals expressed in statutes were little more than pious effusions not intended to have teeth. In any event, regulations, if made, give scope for more detail than is appropriate in an Act of Parliament.

I say "if made" because it is by no means unknown for Ministers to provide in bills for the making of regulations, as a sop to opponents, with no intention of making any. It is not so in this case. In recent times we have witnessed not only a significant development of environmental law, but also a significant development in the attitude of our lords and masters and their civil servants towards conservation. Pious sections genuflecting towards conservation have given place to enforceable duties. Impious failure to enforce inconvenient laws has become a disgraceful chapter of past history.

(a) A sad story

We have long had environmental laws in Britain. They have not always been enforced. We can point to the history of our statutory pollution laws to illustrate the change of attitude towards conservation. Shameful though the story is, it has a happy ending.

Since the stench from the Thames at Westminster compelled Parliament to enact the public health laws of 1875, strong laws against polluters

3

have been on the statute book. Improvements in sewage disposal there were, but during the following century our rivers continued to deteriorate. For too much of the period the enforcement of the laws against polluters fell to the biggest polluters of all, the sewerage authorities. Not surprisingly, enforcement was weak, quantities of polluting effluent were poured into rivers unchecked, and it was left to the common law, at the suit of litigants, to be the most effective weapon against polluters.

Take a typical example. In 1948 pollution of the River Lee from the Luton sewage works was so bad that the owner of a fishery extending from six to nine miles downstream of them obtained an injunction against the Corporation (*Brocket* v *Luton Corporation* [1948] WN 352). The Corporation's eye and mind were so blind to its unlawful fouling of the river that the Town Clerk wrote to the plaintiff, shortly before the writ was served, "There is not, and never has been, pollution of the River Lee by sewage emanating from the Luton Corporation Sewage Works". Mr Justice Vaisey responded to this in his judgment, saying, "any person with eyes and a nose would have been certain in his own mind that here is a dirty river, a river of foul water, with an unpleasant smell, frothy and unclean", and he found the Corporation "almost entirely, if not entirely, responsible".

Thereafter so many polluting Goliaths were slain with the weapon of the common law at the instance of the Anglers' Cooperative Association, that the principal polluters (sewage authorities and industry) lobbied to prevent courts issuing injunctions against them. A clause weakening the power of the courts to do this was included in a government bill rejoicing in the name Protection of the Environment Bill. It took an ambush in the House of Lords, organised by the Country Landowners' Association, to defeat the Government and remove the clause. As it happened, the Bill did not reach the statute book before the 1974 General Election, but the Labour Party, unexpectedly in power with hardly a bill ready, picked it up (shorn of the clause against injunctions) and reinstated it under a different name. It was enacted as the Control of Pollution Act 1974, requiring public registers to be opened detailing discharges of effluent into waters, allowing challenges to discharge consents, and including many other new safeguards.

This measure, proclaimed by Ministers of Conservative and Labour Governments alike, as the one which was going to clean up our rivers, needed Ministerial orders to bring it into force. The polluters lobby, including the regional water authorities responsible for pollution control, regirded their loins, and to such effect that it was a further 11 years before Part II of the Act, strengthening the law against water polluters, was brought into force! Such was the commitment to the protection of the environment by successive governments.

(b) The new dawn

Then the pendulum swung. As recorded in Chapter 6, in 1989 the water industry was privatised. Pollution control was placed in the hands of the National Rivers Authority, a new body with no vested interest in polluting, which proclaimed the dawn of a new era by launching on its first day a criminal prosecution against a major polluter. Many other prosecutions have followed.

4. A balance in the countryside

Rivers and lakes are priceless national assets in any country. In the UK, as elsewhere, they are attractive amenities for people to enjoy. They are also drains and sources of water supply. Pure water is one of the essentials of life, and one of the most important arms of environmental law aims to see that our natural water resources are kept clean and are not depleted. It requires a careful balancing act to meet the needs of water supply, farming and other water-using industries, recreation and aestheticism without killing the geese that lay the golden eggs.

This kind of balancing act has to be performed in all forms of conservation law in the countryside. The countryside is at once a great treasure of natural and man-made beauty, the location of historic sites, monuments and fine architecture, the storehouse of valuable resources of water, timber and minerals, the habitat of wildlife, the playground of people, the shop floor of the farmer and the dwellingplace of millions. It is living and ever changing like the very seasons themselves, whose annual kaleidoscope is best understood by country folk.

Conservation law must recognise this mutability. Planning authorities must understand it. Some creatures live for but a day. Much flora takes life and dies through the seasons of one year, no more. Trees may live for centuries, but healthy forests and woodlands benefit from the forester's selective saw, and many an animal population from nature's or man's culling. The countryside is the source of livelihood for a substantial part of the population and the provider of food required by people, beasts and the national economy. A viable rural economy is essential for the care of the countryside and for sustaining its villages, its produce and its crafts. This is reflected in the balance that the Minister of Agriculture is told by the Agriculture Act 1986, s 17 to aim for, noted under "Agriculture" below. There is no place in countryside law for the absolute preservationist, nurtured in a town centre, admitting no development and apparently seeing no place for mere human beings in the rural environment.

Sir Edward Greenfield put the point neatly when addressing a fringe meeting at the 1992 Party Conference of the Liberal Democrats. He said, "The countryside which we know and love has not evolved by a fluke of nature. Those who feel it should be treated like a museum exhibit, protected by glass screens and viewed by appointment, are sadly mistaken".

The law must be flexible to recognise that human life goes on. Only to a small degree can it be rigid. It can and does outlaw the use of certain hazardous substances and severely restricts the use of others. CFCs (chlorofluorocarbons), which deplete the ozone layer, are to be

5

phased out altogether. Otherwise, practically every rule will be found to have exceptions in order to be realistic and workable.

The general scheme of English environmental law is to control, regulate and manage activities through agencies charged with the duty to protect the environment, backed up with criminal sanctions. Some are given powers by town and country planning statutes, others by specifically environmental measures, such as the Wildlife and Countryside Act 1981, or the Ancient Monuments and Architectural Areas Act 1979. Chapter 2 describes the bodies responsible for conservation. Those closest to the ground are the local authorities, and the Conservancies and Countryside Councils which were invented or reshaped by the Environmental Protection Act 1990 and which carry forward the good work instigated by the National Parks and Access to the Countryside Act 1949. At the same time, in general, public servants, public authorities and bodies, and others officially authorised to undertake services now carry by law a general conservation obligation, and frequently specific conservation duties.

5. Conservation duties

The Countryside Act 1968 showed the way with a sweep of a broad brush. Section 11 laid down:

"In the exercise of their functions relating to land under any enactment every Minister, government department and public body shall have regard to the desirability of conserving the natural beauty and amenity of the countryside".

The Gas Act 1986, privatising the gas industry, brought British Gas plc, and any other authorised public gas supplier, under this section, and the Electricity Act 1989 did likewise for licensed electricity suppliers. In 1968, and for many years after, the duty in section 11 was not taken as seriously as it is now (evidenced by the sad story of pollution related above), but increasingly in the last two decades statutes required statutory bodies and others, with varying degrees of compunction, to pay regard to the conservation of "flora, fauna and geological or physiographical features of special interest". This phrase has become a refrain.

(a) The water law reform

As conservation policies became more insistent, conservation sections in statutes became more elaborate, until we find, in the great reform of the water regime, Acts with pages of statutory provisions devoted to conservation. In the Water Resources Act 1991, s 16 the various Ministers and the National Rivers Authority, in exercising their powers with regard to proposals formulated or considered under the Act, are enjoined:

"(a) . . . to further the conservation and enhancement of natural beauty and the conservation of flora, fauna and geological or physiographical features of special interest; (b) to have regard to the desirability of protecting and conserving buildings, sites and objects of archaeological, architectural or historic interest; and (c) to take account of any effect which the proposals would have on the beauty or amenity of any rural or urban area, or on any such flora, fauna, features, buildings, sites or objects".

Section 16(3) spells it out in greater detail. Section 17 contains safeguards for sites of special scientific interest and section 18 provides for Codes of Practice with regard to environmental duties.

The Water Industry Act 1991, s 3 places the same obligation on the Secretary of State, the Minister of Agriculture, Fisheries and Food, the Director General of Water Services and water undertakers, and the Statutory Water Companies Act 1991 carries it on. The significance of this revolutionary reform of water law, which history will undoubtedly show put an end to "the bad old days" of dereliction of duty by the pollution and water abstraction authorities, is dealt with in Chapter 6. It has become the habit of politicians to change or abolish systems that work well, and it must be hoped the impetus of the National Rivers Authority will not be weakened by the creation of the proposed new environment agency.

6. Agriculture

By 1986 the stock conservation provisions in statutes were no longer pious lip service, but were affecting public policies of Ministries. Agriculture being the primary use of rural land (90 per cent of the surface of Britain is farm land), it is instructive to examine the position of the Ministry of Agriculture, Fisheries and Food (MAFF) in this respect. For long MAFF considered its responsibility went no further than the production and marketing of food. The Agriculture Act 1986 was something of a ragbag of measures, but it took MAFF into new fields. By section 1 the Department's role was expanded. It allowed it to supply "any services and goods" to any person relating to:

(a) production and marketing of produce;
(b) the conservation and enhancement of the natural beauty and amenity of the countryside; or
(c) activities or enterprises of benefit to the rural community.

By section 1(2) its services could be, among other things, by way of information, advice, training, and research and development.

The Act has a later portion under the heading "Conservation". Here can be found section 17 requiring the Minister "in discharging any functions connected with agriculture in relation to any land", to achieve a reasonable balance between four factors. They are:

(1) an efficient agricultural industry;
(2) the economic and social interests of rural areas;

(3) conservation (in accordance with the refrain referred to above); and

(4) the enjoyment of the countryside by the public.

There follows the power to designate environmentally sensitive areas in England and Wales (s 18, see Chapters 3 and 5) and in Scotland (s 19).

MAFF responded positively to its enlarged remit in the Agriculture Act 1986, introducing enterprising new schemes and services, referred to in later chapters. Evidence that it takes its conservation duty seriously can be seen by its range of environmental publications, in the series *Environment Matters*, for the guidance of owners and occupiers of agricultural land, its several Codes of Good Agricultural Practice, its research and development activities and, possibly clearest of all, by the way it administers grant-aid.

(a) "Cross compliance"

Capital grants are available under schemes to help and encourage farmers to diversify, to set aside productive land and to plant woodlands. The principle adopted by MAFF in giving grant-aid is that there must be "cross compliance". By cross compliance, payments are made on condition that the farmer takes steps under the scheme for the protection of the environment.

(b) Farming and Wildlife Advisory Group

Reference has been made above to the need to win hearts and minds if conservation law is to be effective. It should not be overlooked that in agriculture none has done so much in this respect as a voluntary organisation, the Farming and Wildlife Advisory Group (FWAG). Its address is worth noting—Farming & Wildlife Trust Ltd, National Agricultural Centre, Stoneleigh, Kenilworth, Warwickshire CV8 2RX (tel 0203 696699). FWAG states its philosophy as seeking "to stimulate the management of an attractive, living countryside by encouraging the integration of sustainable farming with the conservation or enhancement of wildlife habitats and landscape, in ways which can benefit everyone". With 65 county advisory groups in the UK, advising thousands of farmers each year, FWAG has been a force for conservation and has given credence to the claim that farmers and landowners are among the finest conservationists.

7. Limitations of the law

Too much must not be expected of conservation laws. The law can influence human behaviour and impose sanctions on unlawful conduct, but in the end statutes are only pieces of paper and implementation is left to the human hand. Authorities and individuals have to make up their minds to care for the environment. As we have noted in the sad story of pollution above, without that will even strong laws can be ineffective for want of enforcement.

(a) Expenditure

The law can also encourage the protection of the countryside by enabling money to be spent on it, either directly by authorities, or by offering grants to individuals and voluntary bodies to carry out environmentally friendly work—for example, for tree and hedge planting; or for repairing ancient monuments—or by compensating farmers for sparing the plough or fertiliser or other profit-making practice, to mention but a few instances. The law may require research by public bodies, or grant-aid research, into, for example, improved practices in farming and in other industries; or for waste disposal; or for conservation. The Countryside Commission gives grants for discovering and recording what heritage features exist in the countryside, and English Heritage gives grants for studying and noting-up historic landscapes.

(b) Judicial review

A promising development alongside the growth of conservation laws has been the flourishing of the judicial review process in the High Court. It is a check on public authorities at the suit of litigants. On the one hand the court can be called upon to see that an authority or Minister performs its or his duty, and on the other hand to see that power is not abused. It is fundamental to the British constitutional system that the judiciary shall be independent of the executive. Judicial review is exercised by the High Court without fear or favour. It constantly takes place in the field of planning and environmental law, so that it has become increasingly more difficult and dangerous for authorities to dodge legal conservation duties imposed on them.

(c) Objectors as watchdogs

The case of *R* v *Poole ex parte Beebee* [1991] LMELR 60 is an example of a judge allowing judicial review on the application of objectors aggrieved by a planning consent. It was a case where the local planning authority gave itself planning permission to build houses in a location designated as a site of special scientific interest. The designation by the Nature Conservancy Council was to protect the habitat of smooth snakes, sand lizards, Dartford warblers and other uncommon birds. The World Wildlife Fund and the British Herpetological Society sought judicial review of the planning consent on the ground that the authority failed to consider the need for an environmental impact assessment. The local planning authority argued that the WWF and the BHS had no legal standing to take the proceedings. Schiemann J decided these bodies had a sufficient interest to apply for judicial review, though he controversially dismissed their application. He accepted that the planning authority had not heeded its duty to obtain an environmental impact assessment, but said he was satisfied that it had considered the environmental impact. The Secretary of State, however, after the case, announced he would use his powers to revoke the planning permission.

Responsible objectors are useful watchdogs. Their barking often draws the attention of officialdom to impending harm to the environment or the attention of the public to shortcomings of officialdom. It is interesting to see that people are encouraged by the Departments of the Environment and National Heritage, and the conservation agencies, to bring to their attention threats to heritage sites or buildings. However, objection by someone or another to virtually every form of development in town or country has become so commonplace that objection is losing its impact. Nevertheless, a service the law can give is an opportunity for objectors to make representations about pending decisions affecting their locality or other interests, and it will be seen in later chapters that it is often a requirement of law that applications to do acts which might be environmentally harmful are given publicity for the very purpose of enabling the public to express views. It should be noted that where there is no procedure for objection, there is nothing to stop objectors making representations, either directly or through their elected representatives in Parliament or on councils. In practice local authorities and Ministers quite often invite public comment on proposals, where there is no legal obligation to do so.

8. Planning control

The control of development has been with us since 1947, and the system is outlined in Chapter 5. Planning authorities are in a key position to protect the environment. They are alerted to areas, sites and buildings worthy of special protection by the various forms of designation considered in this book (mainly in Chapter 3)—notably designations of national parks, areas of outstanding natural beauty, sites of special scientific interest, areas of archaeological importance and nature reserves—and by the listing of buildings and scheduling of ancient monuments. Planning authorities themselves designate conservation areas.

(a) Environmental assessment

A more recent concept, stemming from Europe (Directive 86/337), is the requirement, where a development may have a significant effect on the environment, for planning authorities to consider an environmental assessment before giving planning consent. Environmental assessments are also required, by sundry regulations, before decisions are made for a range of activities not needing planning consent, such as projects for new motorways and trunk roads, overhead power lines and trunk pipelines. The idea was taken back into Parliament when its own Standing Orders were amended in 1991 to require an environmental assessment in the Private Bills procedure.

9. What is conservation?

The nearest we get to a legal definition of conservation is in the Environmental Protection Act 1990, s 131(6). As usual with statutory definitions it is neither a true definition, nor very helpful. It trots out the old refrain, stating "'nature conservation' means the conservation of flora, fauna or geological or physiographical features". The definition is for the purposes of Part VII of the Act under the heading "Nature Conservation In Great Britain And Countryside Matters In Wales".

Section 1 of the Act has a shot at defining "the environment", for the purposes of Part I of the Act which deals with integrated pollution control and air pollution control. It states it "consists of all, or any, of the following media, namely, the air, water and land; and the medium of air includes the air within buildings and the air within other natural or man-made structures above or below ground".

(a) Conflicts

The decisions that have to be made in implementing the laws referred to in this book are frequently difficult. Conflicts are inevitable in trying to protect the environment in a just manner. What some want introduced, restored or preserved, others want out of the way. Wind parks for generating electricity, for instance, raise a conflict between visual amenity and the desirability of generating power by using a renewable resource. A by-pass to relieve chronic traffic congestion at Okehampton in Devon impinged on beautiful countryside. English Heritage is being pressed to underwrite the restoration of the Anderton Boat Lift built to raise barges from the Weaver Navigation to the Trent and Mersey Canal. Most see the lift as a unique engineering feat, but if it were a new project today no doubt it would run into spectacular opposition as a visual intrusion, and one wonders whether it would get planning permission. Public access undeniably can, in places, be the enemy of conservation. The Countryside Commission, part of whose remit is to provide for public enjoyment of the countryside, plays down this conflict, and it is to be hoped that it can for the most part be resolved.

It will be gathered that conservation law aims to be realistic, to recognise the facts of life and death, the need for progress and people's rights, whilst imposing necessary restraints and prohibitions for the benefit of present and future generations. It is not about preservation at all costs, though it includes preservation, but it seeks to protect the environment whilst admitting changes. The law can give powers to protect the environment, but it must leave the authorities to use them with wisdom, and the inhabitants and visitors to play their part with wisdom in protecting the countryside they cherish.

Chapter 2

Responsibility for conservation

Abbreviations in this chapter:

DoE = *Department of the Environment*
MAFF = *Ministry of Agriculture, Fisheries and Food*
NRA = *National Rivers Authority*
EPA 1990 = *Environmental Protection Act 1990*

NB: For the meaning of "Secretary of State", see page 24.

This chapter looks at the principal official bodies responsible for rural conservation. Alongside them are hundreds of others, both statutory and voluntary, too numerous to be described here, though playing a part in the protection of the UK's environmental heritage. Details of them can be found in useful reference works such as *The Green Index* (1990) and *Who's Who in the Environment* compiled by Sarah Cowell (The Environment Council 1990).

The National Parks and Access to the Countryside Act was passed as long ago as 1949 giving a framework for national parks, areas of outstanding natural beauty and sites of special scientific interest, but it was another 30 years before the UK and the EEC saw fit to invest enough resources for significant protection of the environment. In response to public opinion the funding of statutory conservation bodies has steadily increased in recent times. Government departments, local authorities and other creatures of statute are required to operate with a proper regard for environmental protection and they have to budget for it. New statutory nature conservancies for Great Britain, created by the Environmental Protection Act 1990 ("EPA 1990"), came into operation on 1 April 1991 in place of the Nature Conservancy Council. Further changes will result if and when the proposed Environment Agency is created.

A. The Government and conservation

The UK Government has conservation obligations deriving from international treaties, the European Community and national legislation.

1. Treaties

The international treaties and agreements on environmental matters to which the UK is a party are legion. Most are listed in *The Environmental Business Handbook* (Euromonitor 1989). They are not binding in the sense that they can be enforced by court action, or that they can legitimise activities unlawful under the domestic law of states, but the obligations are solemn and they are usually implemented, sooner or later, in legislation or other executive action where necessary.

2. The European Community

(a) EC Law

The UK's membership of the EC makes it subject to Community law. Community law can be enforced against member states by the Court of Justice of the European Communities, and it can be enforced by the English courts in proceedings.

Community law is initiated by the European Commission and adopted by the Council of Ministers. It may be in the form of regulations or directives. A sizeable body of both exists concerning the environment, and more is ever in preparation. Regulations are directly binding as part of English law. Directives, provided they are addressed to the UK, and are clear and certain, bind the Government to do what, if anything, is necessary to achieve the result required by them. Primary or subordinate legislation may then be introduced to Parliament, if needed, or some other executive action taken.

(b) The European Court

The European Court of Justice interprets Community law. There is no appeal from its decisions. It is not to be confused with the European Court of Human Rights, a court recognised by all member states, but created by the Council of Europe, not the EC. The High Court in the UK can, in cases before it, seek "preliminary rulings" on points of Community law from the European Court. An interesting instance occurred in *Walkingshaw* v *Marshall* [1991] SCCR 397. A commercial fisherman was charged with using a type of net made illegal by an order implementing EC Regulation No 171/83 for the conservation of fish. He contended that the order was incompatible with Community law. The Scottish appeal court, before deciding the case, obtained a preliminary ruling from the European Court that the order was compatible.

(c) What can an aggrieved European citizen do?

Individuals or bodies who believe the EC is getting something wrong can lobby UK Ministers (either directly or through their MPs), bearing in mind that UK Ministers are represented on the Council of Ministers. An alternative is to lobby members of the European Parliament. They have access to the Commission and to UK Ministers and can raise issues in the European Parliament. The European Parliament is consulted on EC legislation, but, unlike other parliaments, it does not itself legislate. It advises the Commission and the Council of Ministers, and agrees the EC budget. Unless there is a direct dispute with the Commission, there is virtually no opportunity for citizens to get before the European Court—though grievances against governments on human rights can be taken to the European Court of Human Rights.

If it is contended that the government of a member state is not complying with Community law, representations can be made to the Commission. The Commission can take governments before the European Court. Causes of action in the English courts increasingly involve Community law as part of English law, and litigants can invite courts to obtain "preliminary rulings" from the European Court—as in *Walkingshaw* v *Marshall*, above.

3. National legislation

Central government prepares bills and steers them through Parliament, and Ministers make orders and regulations under powers given by statute. There has been a spate in recent years of legislation for the protection of the environment. Useful, if comparatively minor, measures derive also from private members' bills—such as the Wildlife and Countryside (Amendment) Act 1991 (see Chapter 7) introduced by Donald Coleman MP shortly before he died.

4. Departments of State

The contribution of government departments to conservation includes funding key conservation bodies and research and development projects, grant-aiding schemes (Chapter 9 affords examples), exercising sundry controlling powers and having the last word on byelaws—byelaws need ministerial confirmation. Every Department of State is required to pursue policies for the protection of the environment. The most important for England and Wales are the Department of the Environment (DoE), the Ministry of Agriculture, Fisheries and Food (MAFF), the Department of National Heritage and the Welsh Office.

(a) Department of the Environment

The headquarters of the DoE is at 2 Marsham Street, London SW1P 3EB. Telephone 071–212 3434. There will be a new address as the premises are destined to be demolished. The DoE is an outsize department. Among other things it has general responsibility for town and country planning; local government; housing; pollution control; waste regulation and disposal; water; noise control; and transport. It has duties towards the conservation of the natural and built environment, in particular under the Planning (Listed Buildings and Conservation Areas) Act 1990 and the Planning (Hazardous Substances) Act 1990, but some of these have been watered down (not to say confused) by the creation of the Department of National Heritage as explained below. Its former responsibilities for sport and for the royal palaces and parks have been handed over to the new Department, along with many (but not all) of its functions to do with ancient monuments and historic buildings.

Under the Secretary of State there are separate Ministers for a number of these responsibilities. The Department of Transport is a department within the DoE, and the DoE has several inspectorates and directorates. The Secretary of State has overall responsibility for the statutory conservation bodies referred to below. It funds the English ones and may give directions to any of the nature conservancy councils (EPA 1990, ss 130–133).

The Secretary of State determines policies and plays an active role under conservation legislation, in particular the EPA 1990, the Wildlife & Countryside Acts and the four Planning Acts of 1990 under which the Secretary of State has executive functions and decides appeals. Among recent useful publications the DoE has issued an *Environmental Action Guide for Building and Purchasing Managers* (1991) and supporting Advisory Notes (HMSO) addressed to all involved in commissioning building works or managing property and ancillary services. Conservation advice is contained also in its Planning Policy Guides.

Organisational changes in the DoE are not infrequent. Up-to-date information, names, addresses and telephone numbers for its many parts and branches can be checked in reference books, such as the quarterly publication *Vacher's Parliamentary Companion*.

Enquiries of the Department: Much time can be wasted finding the right civil servant when an enquiry is made to any large Department of State. It helps to have a name to ask for on the telephone—even the wrong one, as the wrong one will usually try to get you the right one. When the right one is tracked down, he or she will probably give his or her direct telephone number on request. *The Civil Service Yearbook* is a useful directory of civil servants and the ministries.

(b) Ministry of Agriculture, Fisheries and Food

The headquarters of MAFF is Whitehall Place, London SW1A 2HH. Telephone 071–270 3000. MAFF's duties were revolutionised by the Agriculture Act 1986 ("the 1986 Act"). The result has been dramatic. No longer is food production its simple target. In addition to the responsibilities described by its name, MAFF now has positive environmental and conservation policies. By section 17 of the 1986 Act the Minister is told to have regard to the conservation and enhancement of the natural beauty and amenity of the countryside (including its fauna, flora and other features) in discharging his agricultural functions, and by section 1 he may (and does) see to the supply of services for these same virtues. MAFF operates the important Agriculture Development and Advisory Service (ADAS), and partly funds the Agricultural and

Food Research Council. On 1 April 1992 ADAS became an executive agency, and land use planning units were established at five MAFF regional service centres.

Its scientific research and development activities assist the agriculture industry in the protection of the countryside environment—on biological control of pests; pest-resistant crop species; reduction of refuse; leaching and emissions; protection of land, water and air from pollution; maintaining biodiversity; conserving landscapes; fish conservation and disease; flood defence; and changes to the global climate. The Department has published Codes of Good Agricultural Practice for the protection of water, soil and air, and for good upland management.

Whereas in times past MAFF's grants were aimed at increasing agricultural production, nowadays they are directed to reducing it and to encouraging the protection of the countryside. The policy of "cross compliance" is increasingly used, whereby payments under schemes are conditional upon the adoption of measures for protecting the environment. The Minister is responsible for designating environmentally sensitive areas (ESAs) in England. In *Our Farming Future* (MAFF, November 1991) the Minister announced the intention to create 12 new ESAs in England. These are in train. MAFF has introduced schemes for farm diversification, set-aside and farm woodlands, and more recently the Countryside Premium Scheme, and the Woodland Premium Scheme (see Chapter 9).

(c) The Welsh Office

The principal address of the Welsh Office is Cathays Park, Cardiff CF4 5PL. Telephone 0222 825111. The Secretary of State for Wales has responsibility, subject to national policies for England and Wales, for many of the matters, as far as they apply in Wales, for which there are separate departments at Whitehall. These include protection of the environment; agriculture; transport; industry; and water. The provisions in the Agriculture Act 1986 for environmental conservation and protection, mentioned above, apply in Wales to the Secretary of State for Wales. The Countryside Council for Wales is funded by the Welsh Office and is accountable to the Secretary of State.

(d) Department of National Heritage

The head office of the Department is Horse Guards Road, London SW1P 3AL. Telephone 071–276 3000. The Department of National Heritage was created after the General Election in 1992. It is headed by a Secretary of State. An innovative task given to it was to set up and run a national lottery. The Department took over functions formerly performed by other departments. Unfortunately, it also overlaps with some of the responsibilities of the Department of the Environment.

The present responsibilities of the new Department are the arts in general, films and broadcasting; the architectural and archaeological heritage;

funding museums and galleries in England, the British Library, the Arts Council of Great Britain and other arts bodies; tourism; the royal palaces and parks; and sport and recreation.

Its obligations towards the conservation of the countryside arise from the Department's remit as regards scheduled monuments, listed buildings, conservation areas and sites of historical, architectural and archaeological importance. These matters, however, are bound up with town and country planning, and it is the Secretary of State for the Environment who oversees planning, who exercises planning functions and under whose umbrella these things have previously fallen. Chapter 8 notes how the two Departments share these responsibilities. As the sharing has all the ingredients for conflict and inefficiency, it is expected that there will be a shake-down in due course, and a more rational arrangement worked out.

5. Local government

Local authorities are creatures of statute. Their powers derive entirely from public, private or local Acts of Parliament. One of the most important is the power to make law by way of byelaws, though they are subject to confirmation by the Secretary of State. Another is the power of compulsory purchase of land and rights over it.

They give important services for environmental protection, backed by statutory powers. Local authorities are planning and highway authorities. Their responsibilities concern housing, litter, waste disposal, public health, public recreation, commons, noise abatement, clean air, public nuisances, building regulation, vermin control, listed buildings, country parks and nature reserves. Most of these duties are partial, or joint, or overlap within the local authority structure or with other public bodies. The web is so tangled, the strands are not to be traced within the confines of this book.

The structure of local government keeps changing, and the main political parties have plans for further alterations. Outside the metropolitan areas local government in England and Wales is currently carried out by 44 county councils, about 450 district councils and several thousand parish councils (community councils in Wales). County councils have impact on the environment as highway authorities, but their responsibility does not extend to motorways and trunk roads. They and district councils have planning functions which determine to an extent the character of the countryside, its landscapes and wildlife. The functions of parish councils are less grandiose, but have local impact within parishes, and the councils are consulted on planning matters.

6. The Nature Conservancies

On 1 April 1991 three new agencies took the place of the Nature Conservancy Council, one each for England, Wales and Scotland, and a Joint Nature Conservation Committee was appointed to work with them and co-ordinate national policies for Great Britain as a whole. They were created under the Environmental Protection Act 1990, Part VII, following the White Paper *This Common Inheritance* (1990), and are funded by central government. The Countryside Commission continues, but in Wales the Countryside Council for Wales took over its duties, properties, rights and liabilities (EPA 1990, ss 130 and 136).

(a) Functions common to all the Conservancy Councils

The three nature conservancy councils carry out in their areas the functions previously falling to the Nature Conservancy Council. They have inherited duties and powers derived from the National Parks and Access to the Countryside Act 1949, the Countryside Acts of 1949 and 1968, the Nature Conservancy Council Act 1973 and the Wildlife and Countryside Act 1981, amended and extended by the midwife of the Councils, the Environmental Protection Act 1990.

The Councils are responsible for nature conservation and fostering the understanding of it (EPA 1990, s 131(1)). "Nature conservation" means the conservation of flora, fauna or geological or physiographical features (s 131(6)). The Councils have responsibility for designating and protecting sites of special scientific interest. The responsibility therefore extends to Ramsar sites (wetlands of international importance) and special protection areas (for protection of wild birds under the EC Wild Birds Directive 1979/409), all of which are sites of special scientific interest. They advise the Secretary of State on designation of marine nature reserves, the Agriculture Ministers on environmentally sensitive areas and local authorities on local nature reserves. They advise government Ministers on nature conservation policies in their areas, take responsibility for national nature reserves, give advice and disseminate knowledge on nature conservation to "any person" and commission, support and undertake research. They enter into management agreements with landowners, occupiers and commoners. In carrying out their duties they must have regard to any advice given by the joint committee. They are entitled to own land, or rights over or interests in land and may accept gifts (s 132).

Duties performed and advice given to Ministers affecting Great Britain as a whole, or conservation outside Great Britain, or the establishment of common standards, or joint action by the Councils, are called "special functions" (by EPA 1990, s 133) and may only be performed through the joint committee (s 133). Advice given to the Secretary of State to alter the lists of protected animals or plants in Schedule 5 or 8 to the Wildlife and Countryside Act 1981, or given on quinquennial reviews of the schedules, is a "special function" also. It may only be given jointly by the Councils and through the joint committee (EPA 1990, s 133(2)(a) and Sch 9 paras 5 and 6). The Councils and the joint committee are enjoined "in discharging their nature conservation functions to take appropriate account of actual or possible ecological changes" (s 131(2)).

(b) English Nature

English Nature is the name adopted for the Nature Conservancy Council for England. Its headquarters is Northminster House, Peterborough PE1 1UA. Telephone 0733 340345. Its many initiatives include the Wildlife Enhancement, Nature Conservation, Community Action for Wildlife, Living Churchyard, Volunteer Action and Schools grant schemes, the Species Recovery Programme, and voluntary wardens' awards. Some of these are described in Chapter 9.

(c) Countryside Council for Wales (Cyngor Cefn Gwlad Cymru)

The head office of the Council is at Plas Penrhos, Fford Penrhos, Bangor, Gwynedd LL57 2LQ. Telephone 0248 370444. The Council took over the functions previously performed in Wales by the Nature Conservancy Council and the Countryside Commission. Its remit is therefore wider than that of English Nature, as its responsibilities include, in addition to nature conservation duties, the enhancement of the beauty of the countryside, and getting access opportunities for the public to enjoy open air recreation (EPA 1990, s 130).

Its scope within Wales for giving advice and grants extends to management agreements with owners and occupiers, landscaping projects, recreational facilities and public path development, among other things. It can designate areas as national parks (Wales already has three), as explained in Chapter 3.

The Council is funded by the Welsh Office.

(d) Joint Nature Conservation Committee

The address of the Committee is Monkstone House, City Road, Peterborough PE1 1JY. Telephone 0733 62626. It is a committee of the three nature conservancy councils for England, Wales and Scotland with members from Northern Ireland and the Countryside Commission. As seen above, the Committee is in place to achieve uniformity of national policies within, and to be the agency for nature conservation matters outside, Great Britain, and in particular to ensure that the same scientific standards are adopted throughout by the three conservancy councils.

(e) The Nature Conservancy Council for Scotland

The head office of this Council is at 12 Hope Terrace, Edinburgh EH9 2AS. In 1992 it merged with the Countryside Commission for Scotland to form Scottish Natural Heritage. Its work is not within the scope of this book.

(f) The Countryside Commission

The head office of the Countryside Commission is at John Dower House, Crescent Place, Cheltenham, Gloucestershire GL50 3RA. Telephone 0242

521381. The purpose of the Commission is to conserve and enhance the beauty of the English countryside and to give people better opportunities to enjoy it. It succeeded the National Parks Commission in 1968, but with duties and powers extending to the whole of the English and Welsh countryside. On 1 April 1991 its responsibilities for Wales were handed over to the Countryside Council for Wales. The Commission is funded by the DoE.

The activities of the Countryside Commission include the designation of national parks and areas of outstanding natural beauty, defining heritage coasts and establishing national trails for walkers and riders. It advises the Government and others on countryside matters, is a source of technical advice on conservation and recreation for land managers of all kinds and undertakes research. A wide range of publications are issued. It owns none of the countryside.

The Commission is creating the National Forest in the Midlands, to cover some 150 sq miles and to contain 30 million trees. Community forests are created in co-operation with the Forestry Commission. Three are under way. Nine more are programmed.

Grants are made to promote countryside conservation, public access and recreation. The Commission has instituted the Countryside Stewardship, Countryside Premium, and Rural Action schemes among its many initiatives (see Chapter 9).

Although the Countryside Commission nowadays seeks to achieve results by fostering co-operation and understanding (it was not always thus), it has proved that it is prepared to oppose projects, whether official or private, that it considers harmful to the countryside.

7. English Heritage

English Heritage is the adopted name of the Historic Buildings and Monuments Commission for England. Its head office is currently Fortress House, 23 Savile Row, London W1X 2HE. Telephone 071–973 3000. It may move out of London. The general functions of English Heritage are set out in the National Heritage Act 1983, added to by the Planning and Compensation Act 1991, s 29 and it has powers and duties under other Acts, as referred to in Chapter 8. It is responsible for promoting the preservation and public appreciation of England's archaeological heritage and built environment, and it is making strides with its Monument Protection Programme. It advises the Secretary of State on scheduling ancient monuments and on granting or refusing proposals to repair them, and advises on developments that might damage or destroy them. Advice is also given on listed buildings. The advice of English Heritage is not limited to public authorities, but is offered also to owners and occupiers of land, developers and others.

English Heritage assists owners and occupiers of land to look after ancient monuments under management agreements, makes church grants for major repairs to religious buildings of outstanding historical or architectural interest and makes grants to farmers for surveying their land to identify historic features with the intention of displaying them to the public as an agricultural diversification scheme.

The Commission is preparing a register of landscapes of historic importance. It holds and manages properties of its own. Chapter 8 deals with its work in more detail.

8. Cadw (Welsh Historic Monuments)

Cadw performs in Wales functions similar to English Heritage in England. Its head office is Brunel House, 2 Fitzallan Road, Cardiff CF2 1UY. Telephone 0222 465511.

9. The Forestry Commission

The Forestry Commission headquarters is at 231 Corstorphine Road, Edinburgh EH12 7AT. Telephone 031–334 0303. The Commission is a statutory body founded in 1919 to be responsible for national timber production. From 1 April 1992 the Commission divided into two separate operating units, the Forestry Authority, dealing with grants for and guidance on management and conservation of private woodlands, and Forestry Enterprise, administering the Commission's own forests and timber production.

Some 10 per cent of the land in the UK is forest or woodland. The Commission owns and manages nigh on three million acres and exercises controls on and advises owners of most of the privately owned woodlands. The Forestry Commission therefore stands in an influential position as regards conservation.

The Forestry Act 1967 provides in section 1(2) "The Commissioners shall be charged with the general duty of promoting the interests of forestry, the development of afforestation and the production and supply of timber and other forest products in Great Britain", and adds in section 1(3) "The general duty includes that of promoting the establishment and maintenance in Great Britain of adequate reserves of growing trees". They are also to provide outdoor recreation. By section 1(4) the Commissioners must comply with any directions given to them by the Minister of Agriculture or the Secretaries of State for Wales and Scotland.

A statutory duty is placed on the Forestry Commissioners by the Wildlife and Countryside (Amendment) Act 1985, s 4, to "endeavour to achieve a reasonable balance" between the development of afforestation, management of forests and timber supply, and the conservation and enhancement of natural beauty, flora, fauna and geological and physiographical features of special interest. The Commission has statutory regional advisory committees. These were strengthened by the Forestry Act 1991. The jurisdiction of the Forestry Commission extends to Scotland as well as England and Wales.

The advancement of good silvicultural practices is fostered by education and advice and by conditions attached to the Commission's arrangements with the private sector. Supervision of private forestry is achieved by the Commission's longstanding dedication scheme, by felling control and by grant schemes. Vast areas of private woodlands have been dedicated permanently to forestry subject to plans of operation agreed with the Commission in return for contributions towards expenses. The dedication scheme was closed to new applications in 1981.

Felling control is explained in Chapter 5. The making of grants under the woodland grant scheme and the farm woodland premium scheme is explained in Chapter 9. The schemes are designed to ensure good silvicultural practices, proper landscaping, regard for amenity and conservation and consultation with relevant authorities such as local authorities, the Agriculture Departments, the area Nature Conservancy Council, Countryside Commission and Red Deer Commission. Broadleaf plantings are encouraged by a higher rate of grant. The Environmental Assessment (Afforestation) Regulations 1988 (SI 1988 No 1207), implementing EC Directive 85/337, prohibit the Forestry Commission from making a grant or loan for any afforestation project likely to have significant effects on the environment and which may lead to adverse ecological changes, unless it first takes into consideration environmental information regarding the project. The Regulations set out the procedures to be followed and the content required in any environmental statements prepared by applicants for the financial aid.

10. National Trust

The head office of the National Trust for Places of Historic Interest or Natural Beauty is at 36 Queen Anne's Gate, London SW1H 9AS. Telephone 071-222 9251. The Trust is one of the nation's longest serving and most successful conservation bodies. Although it started as a voluntary enterprise in 1895, it is established and regulated by statute—the National Trust Acts 1907-1971—for "promoting the permanent preservation for the benefit of the nation of lands and tenements (including buildings) of beauty or historic interest and as regards lands for the preservation (so far as practicable) of their natural aspect, features and animal and plant life" (1907 Act).

The National Trust has acquired an estate of over 565,000 acres from gifts of properties ranging from historic houses and gardens to stretches of coastline. The gifts are sometimes coupled with a sum of money for maintenance, and an agreement to allow the donor to remain in occupation.

11. National Rivers Authority

The head office of the National Rivers Authority (NRA) is 30-34 Albert Embankment, London SE1 7TL. Telephone 071-820 0101. The NRA was established by the Water Act 1989 with the main task to protect and improve the water environment in England and Wales and to provide protection against flooding from rivers and the sea. Chapter 6 deals more fully with its powers and duties. They are now found in the Water Resources Act 1991.

It is not an overstatement to say that the institution of the NRA in 1989, on the privatisation of the water industry, was a revolutionary reform for effective and impartial control of water pollution and abstraction, never before attained.

The NRA is expected to be subsumed in the projected new Environment Agency.

12. Her Majesty's Inspectorate of Pollution

The Inspectorate is part of the Department of the Environment (see above). It was formed in 1987 by amalgamating the three Inspectorates for Air Pollution, Radioactive Substances and Hazardous Wastes. Its early days were troubled and its future is uncertain in view of the proposals for an Environment Agency and the fact that the NRA has control of water pollution. Its functions in respect of hazardous industrial processes and dangerous substances are, however, of the utmost importance. Chapter 4 deals with these issues and with the aim for integrated pollution control under the EPA 1990.

13. Some other useful bodies

(a) Broads Authority

Thomas Harvey House, 18 Colegate, Norwich NR3 1BQ. Telephone 0603 610734. Set up by the Norfolk and Suffolk Broads Act 1988 for the protection of the Broads, the Authority is the equivalent of a national park authority and the Broads a national park (see Chapter 3).

(b) British Waterways Board

Greycaine Road, Watford WD2 4JR. Telephone 0923 226422. The Board is responsible for over 2,000 miles of canals and other inland waterways in Great Britain (see Chapter 6).

(c) Inland Waterways Amenity Advisory Council

36 St Paul's Square, Birmingham B3 1QX. Telephone 021–212 1333. The Council advises the British Waterways Board and Ministers under the Transport Act 1968, s 110 on amenity and recreational issues concerning the waterways within the jurisdiction of the British Waterways Board, including their use, wildlife, recreation and conservation of the heritage (see Chapter 6).

(d) Farming and Wildlife Trust

National Agriculture Centre, Stoneleigh, Kenilworth, Warwickshire CV8 2RX. Telephone 0203 696699. With its Farming and Wildlife Advisory

23

Groups this voluntary trust promotes the management of an attractive living countryside by encouraging the integration of sustainable farming with the conservation or enhancement of wildlife habitats and landscape.

(e) The Rural Development Commission

141 Castle Street, Salisbury, Wiltshire SP1 3TP. Telephone 0722 336255. The Commission promotes the well-being of the rural economy by assisting rural businesses, employment, housing and the use of redundant buildings (see Chapter 9).

(f) Royal Society for the Protection of Birds

The Lodge, Sandy, Bedfordshire SG19 2DL. Telephone 0767 680551. Among many activities for the conservation and protection of wild birds the Society owns and manages nature reserves.

* * *

"Secretary of State": Much of the legislation dealt with in this book refers to powers of "the Secretary of State", as if there was but one such dignitary. In reality it is an omnibus term, defined in the Interpretation Act 1978, s 5 and Sch 1 to mean "any of Her Majesty's Principal Secretaries of State". In this book the Secretary of State concerned will usually be the Secretary of State for the Environment, but sometimes the Secretary of State for National Heritage, and usually the Secretary of State for Wales where the locality concerned is wholly in the Principality.

Chapter 3

Designated areas in the countryside

Abbreviations in this chapter:

AONB	= *Area of outstanding natural beauty*
ESA	= *Environmentally sensitive area*
NNR	= *National nature reserve*
SSSI	= *Site of special scientific interest*
The Welsh Council	= *The Countryside Council for Wales*
1949 Act	= *National Parks and Access to the Countryside Act 1949*
W&CA 1981	= *Wildlife and Countryside Act 1981*
A conservancy, or,	
the conservancies	= *English Nature and/or the Welsh Council*

NB: For the meaning of "Secretary of State", see page 24.

A large proportion of the countryside of England and Wales is within areas designated under one legal umbrella or another as being especially beautiful, historic, interesting or otherwise desirable to be conserved, or kept available for public access. The White Paper *This Common Inheritance* (Cm 1200 HMSO) in September 1990 recorded that national parks and land under the jurisdiction of the Broads Authority together covered 9 per cent of the land mass of England and Wales, areas of outstanding natural beauty (AONBs) covered a further 13 per cent, over 3,500 sites of special scientific interest (SSSIs) covered 7 per cent of Great Britain, and 790,000 hectares were in environmentally sensitive areas (ESAs). In addition, there were 7,500 conservation areas, 21,000 scheduled monuments, 500,000 listed buildings, 146 national nature reserves, 230 local nature reserves and two marine nature reserves. Since then, another 12 ESAs have been designated or announced, and 5 more NNRs created.

This chapter examines what these and some other forms of designation are, and their significance for conservation. Some of them have been around since the National Parks and Access to the Countryside Act 1949 ("the 1949 Act"). In those early days they were somewhat pious conceptions, the legislation having few teeth and the authorities scant resources. As time has gone on, controls, constraints and new forms

25

of designation have multiplied ensuring that designated areas will be truly significant for conservation. At the same time the rural economy is to be protected. The Countryside Act 1968, s 37, places a duty on Ministers and the statutory bodies exercising functions under the Act and the 1949 Act "to have due regard to the needs of agriculture and forestry and to the economic and social interests of rural areas".

1. National parks

Presently there are ten national parks in England and Wales. Seven are in England—the Peak District, the Lake District, Northumberland National Park, the North York Moors, the Yorkshire Dales, Dartmoor and Exmoor—and Wales has the Pembrokeshire Coast, Snowdonia and the Brecon Beacons. These ten parks were all designated between 1951 and 1957 by the sometime National Parks Commission. Their combined area is 13,618 sq km. The 1949 Act, as amended and extended by the Countryside Act 1968 (both Acts amended by later legislation), is still the basis of the law for national parks.

(a) The Broads

The Norfolk and Suffolk Broads are not a national park but they have their own regulating legislation (the Norfolk and Suffolk Broads Act 1988, a local Act) and Broads Authority, giving the area the equivalent status of a national park. The Act stipulates that the Broads Authority is to be treated as a national park authority for the purposes of the Wildlife and Countryside Act 1981 and of sections 64, 65 and 77 of the 1949 Act. This formula of tailor-made legislation is to be followed in designating 200 sq miles of The New Forest as "an area of national significance", indicating a belief that the creation of a discrete framework is better than using the higgledy-piggledy arrangements for national parks.

(b) The pedigree of national parks

The campaign to create national parks goes back to the nineteenth century. It gained ground when the Addison Report recommended their formation in 1931. Other official reports and a White Paper (*Control of Land Use*, Cmnd 6537 in 1944) followed. Not until 1949 did the National Parks and Access to the Countryside Act create the National Parks Commission with power to designate national parks, and the ten were then designated. The Commission's functions were enlarged by the Countryside Act 1968 and its name changed to the Countryside Commission. Until 1 April 1991 the Commission operated in England and Wales. On that date its functions in Wales were handed over to the Countryside Council for Wales ("the Welsh Council") in accordance with the revised system for conservation introduced by the Environmental Protection Act 1990 described in Chapter 2.

(c) Purposes of national parks

The 1949 Act stated that its provisions for national parks had the purpose of "preserving and enhancing the natural beauty of the areas" so designated and "promoting their enjoyment for the public" (s 5(1)). These areas are, in the words of section 5(2):

> "extensive tracts of country in England and Wales as to which it appears to the Commission that by reason of their natural beauty and the opportunities they afford for open air recreation, having regard to their character and to their position in relation to centres of population, it is especially desirable that the necessary measures shall be taken for the purposes mentioned".

The expression "open air recreation" does not include organised games, says the Act (s 114(1)). "The Commission" in the 1949 Act and in the Countryside Act 1968 now means the Countryside Commission as regards areas in England, and the Welsh Council as far as Wales is concerned.

Further changes are in the offing. The National Parks Review Panel's Report *Fit for the Future* (1991) made numerous recommendations which it suggested should be included in a new National Parks Act. The Panel recommended that the purposes of national parks should be:

> "(i) to protect, maintain and enhance the scenic beauty, natural systems and land forms, and the wildlife and cultural heritage of the area; and (ii) to promote the quiet enjoyment and understanding of the area, insofar as it is not in conflict with the primary purpose of conservation".

It called for independent authorities with planning powers for each park; and also for each park, environmental inventories; nature conservation strategies; restrictions on noisy recreation; greater research; traffic management policies; a ban on new coniferous afforestation; incentives to farmers and landowners to achieve national park objectives; coupling environmental assessments to planning applications; and much more. The Countryside Commission's *Agenda for the Countryside* (1991) envisages many of these reforms taking place.

(d) Designation

National parks are created by the Commission, or the Welsh Council, designating areas as such and the Secretary of State of the Environment confirming the designation under the 1949 Act. Before designation there must be consultation with every local authority affected, and publicity given to the proposal. It is in no sense a nationalisation of the land. The process involves no change of ownership, occupation or use of the land. It is mainly privately owned, occupied, lived in and worked.

27

(e) Restraints on land use

The Commission and the Welsh Council do not wave big sticks. They have none to wave, being primarily advisory and not executive bodies. Nevertheless, restraints on land use are achieved in practice by the park authorities. The restraints mainly derive from the planning process, and the somewhat limited power to make byelaws.

The policy of conserving the natural beauty of the national parks is sought to be achieved in the following ways.

(i) Planning authorities employ a policy of planning restraint for land in national parks.

(ii) Many of the exemptions from planning control in the General Development Order 1988, SI 1988 No 1813 (as amended, see Chapter 5), do not apply in national parks and the Broads, nor in areas of outstanding natural beauty, dealt with below. They are "Article 1(5) land". A summary can be found in the department of the Environment Planning Policy Guide PPG7 (January 1992). The modification of permitted development rights includes lower size-limits free from planning control on extensions to domestic and industrial buildings, and planning permission is required for certain alterations and installations affecting the appearance of buildings, which are exempt from planning control outside the designated areas; and in national parks and the Broads (though not AONBs) extensions and alterations to agricultural buildings permitted by the General Development Order are subject to siting and design control, and excavations for fish farms need planning consent.

(iii) Moorland and heath in national parks may be given special protection by the making of moorland orders (see below).

(iv) Local authorities, the Commission and the Welsh Council can use byelaw-making powers for land or waterways in or adjacent to national parks, or AONBs under access agreements, for the preservation of order, the prevention of damage and for securing that visitors do not interfere with the enjoyment by others of the land or waterways (1949 Act, s 90 and see Countryside Act 1968, s 41). Wardens may be appointed to advise and assist the public (s 92 and Wildlife and Countryside Act 1981, s 49).

(v) Park authorities are appointed to prepare and implement management plans, and are required by the Planning and Compensation Act 1991 to prepare local plans for the whole of their areas and also policies for minerals and waste.

(vi) Management agreements are made with owners and occupiers of land, controlling land use, as described in Chapter 5.

(f) Management of national parks by park authorities

Oddly, the park authorities are independent boards in some instances and committees of local authorities in others. The Peak Park has an independent Joint Planning Board and the Lake District an independent

Special Planning Board. The remaining national parks have park planning committees. Where the park is in more than one county it is a joint committee. The anomalous distinction will disappear if the recommendations of the 1991 report of the National Parks Review Panel are adopted.

The boards and park planning committees exercise the development control functions of county and district planning authorities for the area of their parks, in accordance with their local plans. The jurisdiction of the local planning authorities is diminished accordingly. An important difference between park authorities is that the boards, but not the park planning committees, fund their expenses by a precept on the district councils. The committees have to indent for their budget to the finance committees of the local authorities, which decide how much they may spend.

Membership of the park authorities (boards and committees) is appointed as to one-third by the Secretary of State for the Environment, after consultation with the Commission or Welsh Council, and the remainder by the local authorities under rules set out in the Local Government Act 1972, Sch 17 (as amended by the W&CA 1981, s 46).

(g) Moorland and heathland orders

Power is given to Ministers to restrain the ploughing of moorland and heathland in national parks by making orders with criminal sanctions. The power is in the W&CA 1981, s 42. The Act repealed an earlier provision in the Countryside Act 1968, s 14. The "Ministers" are the Minister of Agriculture, Fisheries and Food, or—in Wales or Scotland— the Secretary of State.

Orders may be made for land in national parks consisting of, or including, moor or heath which has not been agricultural land within the preceding 20 years. It is an offence "without reasonable excuse" to plough or otherwise convert the land into agricultural land, or to carry out any other agricultural or forestry operation, specified in the order, likely to affect the character or appearance of the moor or heath land.

As with some other designations, the system is designed to buy time to negotiate a management agreement with farmers. An offence is not committed if the owner or occupier gives the county planning authority written notice of a proposal to carry out prohibited operations, and either:

   (i)   the authority consents; or

   (ii) where consent is neither given nor refused, three months have expired since the notice; or

   (iii) where consent has been refused, 12 months have expired since the notice.

A refusal of consent can therefore prohibit the operations for 12 months only, though, as a last resort, the land could be designated an SSSI and purchased compulsorily.

2. Areas of outstanding natural beauty

The 38 AONBs stem from the same campaign and the same legislation as spawned the national parks, described above. Twenty-thousand four-hundred square kilometres of England and Wales are covered by AONBs. The 1949 Act (still, as amended, the basis of the law) describes AONBs as areas not in national parks which are of such outstanding natural beauty that they should be designated as AONBs (ss 87 and 114). Like national parks, designation is by the Countryside Commission for areas in England and by the Welsh Council for areas in Wales, but thereafter the position of the Commission and the Council is advisory rather than executive; and like national parks, land in AONBs is in no sense nationalised, but by and large is privately owned, occupied, lived in and worked.

(a) Purpose of designation

The purpose of designation is to identify, conserve and enhance the beauty of landscapes of outstanding natural beauty. "Natural" must not be taken too literally. Much of the beauty leading to designation may be due to the hand of its owners and occupiers over the years.

(b) Differences between AONBs and national parks

A significant difference is that one of the specified purposes of a national park is to encourage public access. This is not so with AONBs, as appears from section 1 of the 1949 Act (as substituted by the EPA 1990, Sch 8 para 1). The Countryside Commission, however, recognises that "a secondary aim of AONBs is to meet the need for quiet enjoyment of the countryside", and a general duty is placed on the Welsh Council to encourage the enjoyment of the countryside in Wales (Environmental Protection Act 1990, s 130(2)). Public access, of course, can conflict with the aim of conserving the character and wildlife of beautiful countryside.

Another difference is that national parks are intended to be "extensive tracts of country", whilst AONBs may be any area, large or small, remote or populated, of outstanding beauty outside the national parks. An important legal difference is that there are national park authorities of some kind for each park. There are no special statutory arrangements for the administration of AONBs, although the formation of joint advisory committees of local authorities, local people and conservation bodies, is encouraged by the official agencies and endorsed in the Department of the Environment Planning Policy Guide PPG7 (January 1992).

(c) Designation

As in the case of national parks, before the Countryside Commission or Welsh Council designates an area as an AONB, there must first be consultation with the local authorities affected and the proposal must be publicly advertised. Designation requires confirmation by the Secretary of State for the Environment with or without a public inquiry. Although there is an opportunity for representations to be made before confirmation, there is no provision for direct notification of the proposal to owners, occupiers or any voluntary bodies who may be concerned.

(d) Effect of designation

Designation earmarks the area for special attention by the planning authorities and the Countryside Commission, or Welsh Council, for cosseting its natural beauty. Local authorities are given general powers to preserve and enhance the beauty of the area (1949 Act, s 11), but few teeth other than those they already possess.

Restraints on land uses injurious to the aims of AONBs are sought to be achieved in the same way as for national parks as described above, by policies of planning restraint; by certain planning control exemptions not applying to AONBs; by making byelaws and appointing wardens to enforce them (under the 1949 Act, ss 90–92); and by making management agreements with landowners and occupiers.

The function of the Countryside Commission and the Welsh Council is advisory and exhortative, and grant-aid can be given to encourage sympathetic management of land in AONBs. The Countryside Commission states that priority grant-aid is given "for countryside rangers who repair and maintain the countryside's 'fabric', e.g. woodland management, footpath, stile or wall rebuilding, and minimise visitor pressure, e.g. by waymarking, wildlife 'remote zones' and information policies" (brochure: *Areas of Outstanding Natural Beauty in England and Wales*). Advice and grants are available to landowners and farmers for landscape conservation and enhancement under management agreements and other schemes, as noted in Chapter 9.

Planning permission for development (including changes of use) is by no means outlawed in AONBs, but planners adopt a presumption against allowing major developments, and where planning consents are given, they are coupled where necessary with conditions to ensure harmony with the area. The 1949 Act requires planning authorities to consult the Countryside Commission or the Welsh Council on development plan proposals affecting AONBs (see ss 6, 9 and 88).

3. Sites of special scientific interest

(a) Background

The identification of sites of special biological or other scientific importance was recommended by Julian Huxley's Wildlife Conservation Committee reporting in 1947 (*Conservation of Nature in England and Wales*, Cmnd 7122). It was taken up in a half-hearted manner by the 1949 Act which placed a duty on the Nature Conservancy to notify local planning authorities of sites of special biological, geological or physiographical interest (s 23). Not until 36 years later, with the passing of the Wildlife and Countryside (Amendment) Act 1985, did the law develop sufficiently to give a realistic chance of protecting these sites. Until the W&CA 1981 there was, not to put too fine a point on it, much foolishness. Owners and occupiers of sites were not notified of their designation, but were freely castigated for damaging, by farming the land, SSSIs they did not know existed. The spirit of co-operation so common today, was hard to find, but confrontation with, and distrust of, the Nature Conservancy were not. The present system has banished most of the old nonsenses.

(b) Present system

To understand the current system it must be appreciated that it is based on "the voluntary principle", compulsion being not a first but a last resort. The ordinary designation of SSSIs is under section 28 of the W&CA 1981, crucially amended by the Wildlife and Countryside (Amendment) Act 1985. Another procedure is available for protection of sites of extra special importance, by orders under section 29. Sections 28 and 29 of the W&CA 1981 have both been amended by the Environmental Protection Act 1990 to take account of the new regime of nature conservancies.

(c) Notification by conservancies

Section 28 of the W&CA 1981 provides that where English Nature or the Welsh Council ("the conservancies") are of the opinion that any area of land is of special interest by reason of its flora, fauna, or geological or physiographical features, they have a duty to notify the fact to:

(i)   the local planning authority; and
(ii) every owner and occupier of the land; and
(iii) the Secretary of State.

The notification must give at least three months from the date of notification for representations or objections to be made. Notification to owners and occupiers must specify the flora, fauna or feature making the site of special interest, and any operations likely to damage it (s 28(4)). If the conservancy cannot find the name and address of an owner or occupier after reasonable enquiry, notification may be served by addressing it to "the owner" or "the occupier" of the land and affixing it to a conspicuous object on the land (s 28(3)).

The SSSI is legally protected immediately on notification. Before the 1985 amending Act, it was not. Notification was in effect notice of a last chance to plough, drain or carry out any operation about to become prohibited. So notification itself sometimes instigated damage to sites.

After notification of the SSSI the conservancy must confirm or withdraw it within nine months from the date of service on the Secretary of State. It ceases to have effect if not confirmed within nine months.

(d) Notice by owners and occupiers of intended operations

The owner or occupier of the site of an SSSI commits an offence if "without reasonable excuse" he carries out, while the notification is in force, any operation specified in it as potentially damaging, unless he has given the conservancy written notice of a proposal to carry out the operation and one of the following applies:

(i) the conservancy has given written consent; or

(ii) the operation accords with the terms of a management agreement made with the conservancy; or

(iii) four months have expired since the written notice was given to the conservancy (s 28(5), (6)).

The object is to give the conservancy four months to negotiate an arrangement, or to resort to compulsory procedures, if it wants to stop the proposed operation. The four months can be extended by agreement.

(e) "Reasonable excuse"

The W&CA 1981 sets out two reasonable excuses relieving the owner from criminal liability, namely:

(i) the operation was authorised by a planning permission (under the Town and Country Planning Act 1990; or

(ii) the operation was an emergency operation particulars of which (including details of the emergency) were notified to the conservancy as soon as practicable after commencement of the operation (s 28(8)).

It is generally thought that these are the only exceptions, but the wording of section 28(8) ("It is a reasonable excuse in any event . . .") suggests the contrary. In theory, at least, planning consents should not endanger the reasonable protection of SSSIs, because the conservancy must be consulted by the planning authority under the General Development Order 1988 on any application for planning consent involving an SSSI. Should the planners appear bent on allowing a development injurious to an SSSI the conservancy could invite the Secretary of State to "call it in" for his own determination.

(f) Protective action by conservancies

Positive steps can be taken to protect SSSIs by conservancies entering into management agreements with the owners and occupiers of the land under section 15 of the Countryside Act 1968. The conservancies, owners and occupiers may seek management agreements at any time. Normally the conservancy will do so if it wishes to prevent an activity proposed in a notice served by an owner or occupier under section 28(5). The agreement will usually include compensation for loss caused to the owner or occupier by being prevented from carrying out lawful profitable activities—typically agricultural or forestry operations. Where an owner or occupier is refused a farm capital grant by the Ministry of Agriculture, Fisheries and Food only because of an objection from a conservancy, the conservancy is bound to offer a management agreement (s 32).

The conservancies have powers of compulsory purchase of land, or of interests in land they wish to protect under the 1949 Act, s 17. In practice compulsory acquisition is unwanted and is looked upon as a last resort when agreement cannot be reached. A further recourse, in appropriate instances, is to apply to the Secretary of State to make a nature conservation order under section 29 of the W&CA 1981 (see *(h)* below).

(g) The National Rivers Authority, the water industry and SSSIs

In 1991 the High Court quashed a conviction of the Southern Water Authority for damaging the Alverstone Marshes SSSI on the Isle of Wight by drainage operations, holding that the Authority was not an "occupier", even though it was on the land for four weeks, because it had no legal interest in the land (*Nature Conservancy Council* v *Southern Water Authority* (The Times, 17 June 1991)). This is not the loophole it might seem. The prosecution was before the privatisation of the water industry in 1989, and now the National Rivers Authority (successor to the water authorities) has a statutory duty to protect the environment. The conservancies are required to notify the National Rivers Authority of SSSIs that its activities might injure and the National Rivers Authority must then consult the conservancy (except in an emergency) before carrying out or authorising any works or operations likely to destroy or damage a notified SSSI (Water Resources Act 1991, ss 16 and 17). The Water Industry Act 1991, s 4 makes similar provision for the private water undertakers. Failure to consult would be subject to judicial review.

Statutory codes of practice may also be issued by Ministers for adherence by the National Rivers Authority and water plcs with respect to their environmental duties (Water Resources Act 1991, s 18; Water Industry Act 1991, s 5). Contravention of a code does not of itself give rise to criminal or civil liability, but it may be taken into account when Ministers exercise powers.

(h) Nature conservation orders

Nature conservation orders, made under section 29 of the W&CA 1981, are for the protection of extra special sites, sometimes called "super SSSIs". They may be made by the Secretary of State for the Environment, after consultation with the conservancy, to secure the survival in Great Britain of any kind of animal or plant, or to comply with an international obligation. Orders may also be made to conserve any of the flora, fauna or geological or physiographical features of a site of "national importance".

A nature conservation order imposes restrictions on carrying out operations specified in it, and applies to all persons (not just owners and occupiers as under section 28). Procedures for making orders are set out in Schedule 11 to the W&CA 1981. The schedule requires publicity to be given to orders and an opportunity for objections to be made and heard. Orders take effect as soon as they are made, but they must be confirmed by the Secretary of State within nine months, otherwise they lapse.

It is permissible to include in a nature conservation order land which on its own would not be of national importance, if it is part of an environmental unit or habitat which taken as a whole is of national importance (*Sweet* v *Secretary of State* [1989] 2 PLR 14, Schiemann J).

It is an offence for any person to carry out on the land any operation specified in a nature conservation order as likely to damage or destroy the flora, fauna or feature to be protected. On conviction of an offence under section 29 (though not under section 28) the court may order the offender to restore the land to its former condition. Failure to comply is a further offence, and the conservancy may do the restoration itself and recover the reasonable cost from the offender (s 31). The court may also impose an unlimited fine.

The same defences and reasonable excuses apply as for ordinary SSSIs under section 28 above, and the orders are registrable as land charges. As with section 28 procedures, owners and occupiers may give written notice of proposals to carry out specified potentially damaging operations, and the same exempting conditions of consent by the conservancy, planning permission and lapse of time (in this case three months) apply.

A major difference from section 28 SSSI notifications is that the time ban on operations is extended if the conservancy offers to enter into a management agreement within the three months, or offers to acquire the interest of the person who gave notice of the proposal. If the management agreement or agreement to acquire the interest is entered into within 12 months of the owner's or occupier's written notice, the time ban is extended up to the day of the agreement. In any other case the extension is for 12 months from the giving of the notice, or three months from any rejection or withdrawal of the offer to enter into an agreement, whichever is the latest (s 29(6)).

This procedure is designed to protect the site as soon as the section 29 order is made and then to give time to negotiate and conclude an agreement with the owner or occupier, or resort to compulsory purchase if negotiations fail.

Section 30 of the 1981 Act provides for compensation to persons having an interest in an agricultural unit to which a section 29 order relates, equal to any diminution caused to the value of the interest. Where written notice is given by an owner or occupier of a proposal to carry out works prohibited by an NCO, compensation is claimable for expenditure made abortive by the order, or for loss or damage occasioned.

The conservancies have power to enter land to ascertain whether a nature conservation order should be made, or if an offence has been committed (s 51).

4. Nature reserves

Statutory national nature reserves (NNRs) and local nature reserves are from the same stable as SSSIs—the Report of the Wildlife Conservation Special Committee in 1947 and the 1949 Act. The W&CA 1981 later provided for marine nature reserves.

(a) National nature reserves

All NNRs are SSSIs. Until the W&CA 1981 none could be. The Act removed the distinction between them. The 1949 Act provided for the designation of NNRs by the then Nature Conservancy as land managed to provide opportunities, under suitable conditions and control, for study and research into the flora, fauna and geological and physiographical features of the area, or for preserving or protecting them (s 15). The Nature Conservancy was given compulsory purchase powers (s 17), but not the resources to exercise them, and powers to enter into management agreements for the reserves (s 16, and see Countryside Act 1968, s 15). Reserves can be protected by byelaws made under section 19.

By section 35 of the W&CA 1981 a conservancy may declare any land to be an NNR if it is satisfied that it is of national importance and is being managed as a nature reserve either:

(i)   under an agreement with the conservancy; or
(ii) by the conservancy; or
(iii) by a body approved by the conservancy.

The purpose of the declaration is to enable byelaws to be made for its protection.

Most NNRs are not owned by a conservancy, but are managed under agreements with owners, private or public, or leased from them. Some of the most important are owned and managed by the Royal Society for the Protection of Birds. Owners can be compensated for the costs of works undertaken by them, or for loss caused by restrictions on the use of the land in agreements (see W&CA 1981, s 50 for payments).

(b) "Ramsar sites", special protection areas and special areas of conservation

NNRs include "Ramsar sites", selected by the conservancies and designated by the Secretary of State as wetlands of international importance, especially for wildfowl, under the Ramsar Convention 1971, to which Great Britain is a signatory. They also include special protection areas, for safeguarding rare migratory birds under the EC Wild Birds Directive 1979 (79/409). By August 1993, 72 special protection areas had been designated. They are not to be confused with the latest invention, namely special areas of conservation, to be designated under the EC Directive on the Conservation of Natural Habitats and of Wild Fauna and Flora (92/43). As this book goes to press, draft regulations are expected which will require planning authorities, before reaching a decision on any proposed development which may have a significant effect on a special protection area, or a special area of conservation, to assess the implications on the conservation objectives for which the area was designated. After Parliament has considered the draft regulations, but before they come into effect in 1994, the Department of the Environment and the Welsh Office intend to publish a new Planning Policy Guide on Nature Conservation.

(c) Local nature reserves

The 1949 Act gave local authorities powers to establish local nature reserves, where it was considered to be in the local interest to do so, and to protect them by byelaws and to enter into agreements for their management (s 21).

(d) Byelaws

Proper protection of a nature reserve requires control of access. The conservancies have the power to make byelaws to this end (s 20). However, the rights of owners of the land cannot be restricted by byelaws, nor public rights of way, nor the rights of certain public bodies carrying out their statutory functions. Byelaws need to be confirmed by a Minister and they can be set aside by the High Court if they are unreasonable (*Kruse* v *Johnson* [1898] 2 QB 91). Public rights of way are jealously guarded by the law. There are formidable procedures for extinguishing or diverting them under the Highways Act 1980. It is submitted that it cannot reasonably be done by the sidewind of byelaws, and Ministers have declined to confirm byelaws prohibiting the public right of fishing on the foreshore, a right given by Magna Carta 1215. A byelaw forbidding anglers from digging for bait on the foreshore was invalid (*Anderson* v *Alnwick DC* [1993] 1 WLR 1156 (DC)).

(e) Marine nature reserves

The two marine nature reserves (Lundy Island, off Devon, and Skomer-Bardsey Islands, off Wales) are designated under the W&CA 1981, s 36 (amended by the Territorial Sea Act 1987 and the Environmental Protection Act 1990). Under section 36 the Secretary of State, on the application of a conservancy, may designate by order any land covered (continuously or intermittently) by tidal waters or parts of the sea as marine nature reserves to be managed by the conservancy. The purpose is to conserve marine flora, fauna, or geological or physiographical features of special interest, and to provide, under suitable conditions and control, special opportunities for study and research.

Schedule 12 to the W&CA 1981 sets out procedures for making orders. Section 37 gives the conservancies power to make byelaws protecting the reserves. Byelaws may prohibit or restrict entry to the reserve, and prohibit killing, destruction, molestation or disturbance of animals or plants or interference with the sea bed, or the deposit of rubbish. The consent or confirmation of the Secretary of State is needed for byelaws to take effect. A model is the Wildlife and Countryside (Byelaws for Marine Nature Reserves) Regulations 1986 (SI 1986 No 143).

5. Environmentally sensitive areas

A new approach to conservation, quite different from designations under the 1949 Act, was unveiled when ESAs were introduced in 1986. The new concept was to pay farmers for environmental services, instead of relying on planners to inhibit development in designated areas, or hoping to deter transgressions by byelaws.

(a) Background

The Agriculture Act 1986, s 18 enables Ministers to designate ESAs. The section implements the policy of the EC Regulation on Improving the Efficiency of Agricultural Structures 1985, Art 19 (797/85). European funding is available for it. The policy is to contract with farmers to modify their farming so that farming for profitable yields gives place to conservation practices. Initially nineteen ESAs were designated in the UK (including five in Scotland and two in Northern Ireland). A further six were programmed for 1992 and six more for 1993. Typically farmers agree not to plough or drain certain lands, or exceed specified stocking levels, or use fertilisers, herbicides or pesticides, and to adopt positive measures, such as traditional grazing methods and to maintain features such as dry-stone walls, for preserving characteristics of the area.

(b) The scheme for ESAs

Section 18 of the Agriculture Act 1986 provides that if it appears to the Minister particularly desirable to conserve the natural beauty, flora, fauna or geological or physiographical features of an area, or to protect buildings or other objects of archaeological, architectural or historic interest in an area, and that the maintenance or adoption of particular agricultural methods is likely to facilitate such conservation, enhancement or protection, he may, with the consent of the Treasury designate the area as an ESA. "The Minister" is the Minister of Agriculture, Fisheries and Food as regards areas in England, and the Secretary of State for Wales or for Scotland as regards areas in those countries (s 18(11)). Designation is by an order contained in a statutory instrument (s 18(12)). Before making an order the Minister must consult the conservancy for England, Wales or Scotland, as the case may be. The protection of the area is by voluntary agreements. Once an area is designated as an ESA, applications are invited from owners and occupiers of agricultural land in, or partly in, the area, to enter into agreements.

(c) Agreements

The Minister may make an agreement with any person with an interest in the land (including part-time farmers) if he considers it likely to facilitate any of the purposes of the ESA. Each ESA has its own particular environmental objectives. The agreements will require the land to be managed in a manner, specified in the agreement, designed to meet the objectives, in consideration for payments made by the Minister (s 18(3)). The order may specify:

(i)   requirements to be included in agreements as to agricultural practices, methods of operation and the installation or use of equipment;

(ii) the period or minimum period of the agreement (usually a minimum of five years);

(iii) provisions concerning any breach of requirements; and

(iv) the rates or maximum rates of payments (s 18(4)).

An agreement will be binding on, and enforceable against, successors (s 18(7)). Payments are made at a flat rate to reduce administrative costs.

Although the scheme is voluntary, the first ESAs have been pronounced a success by Ministers, environmentalists and farmers. The Pennine Dales ESA, for example, originally attracted 300 agreements covering 9,800 hectares, in consideration of payments at £90 per ha for pastures and £125 per ha for hay meadows, farmed to protect their special habitats, floral diversity and other features. In 1992 the ESA was extended. Payments were increased to ensure that the land could be viably farmed under the agreement restrictions.

6. Some other designations

Other designations can be noted briefly.

(a) Limestone pavement orders

A clause was added during the passage of the Wildlife and Countryside Bill recognising the need to preserve limestone pavements as geologically and physiographically interesting features, valuable as habitats for flora. Section 34 of the 1981 Act places a duty on the conservancies to notify planning authorities of any limestone pavement they consider of special interest. The Secretary of State, or the county planning authority, can then make a limestone pavement order if it appears that the pavement would be likely to be adversely affected by removal or disturbance of the limestone. Procedures are set out in Schedule 11. It is an offence to remove or disturb without reasonable excuse limestone in or on land designated by an order (s 34(4)). Planning permission to do so is a reasonable excuse (s 34(5)).

> "'Limestone pavement' means an area of limestone which lies wholly or partly exposed on the surface of the ground and has been fissured by natural erosion" (s 34(6)).

(b) Nitrate sensitive areas

Areas may be designated as nitrate sensitive areas under the Water Resources Act 1991 where the relevant Minister considers it necessary to prevent or control the entry of nitrate into waters from agricultural land. This is described more fully in Chapter 6.

(c) Conservation areas

Local planning authorities may designate conservation areas under the Planning (Listed Buildings and Conservation Areas) Act 1990 where it is deemed desirable to preserve the character and appearance of buildings or land of historical or architectural interest. The 7,500 conservation areas are virtually all in towns and villages. This is described more fully in Chapter 8.

(d) Country parks

As the object of country parks is to provide for public recreation, they are hardly within the scope of this book. They are mentioned because their existence conserves rural land, and many contain SSSIs. They are created by local authorities under the Countryside Act 1968, ss 6 to 8, to provide public rural pleasure grounds closer to home, for most of the urban population, than national parks, with free admittance.

(e) Heritage coasts

"Heritage coast" is not a statutory designation and there are no laws specifically for the protection of heritage coasts. It is a description given to the most beautiful parts of the coastline of England and Wales to identify them for conservation. Eight hundred and fifty miles of the coastline of England and Wales (31 per cent of it) have been so defined. Most heritage coast is in designated areas of outstanding natural beauty or national parks, and 29 per cent of heritage coastline is safeguarded by the ownership of the National Trust. Some of the rest is local authority owned. The Crown owns much of the foreshore, but a great deal of the land involved is privately owned. Planning control is a tool against undesirable development. Positive management is sponsored by funding from the conservancies.

(f) Areas of great landscape value

This is not a statutory designation, but such areas are usefully identified by planning authorities in local plans and structure plans for protection against spoliation by development.

Chapter 4

Tackling nuisances and dangers

Abbreviations in this chapter:

GMO	*= Genetically modified organism*
HMIP	*= Her Majesty's Inspectorate of Pollution*
COPA 1974	*= Control of Pollution Act 1974*
EPA 1990	*= Environmental Protection Act 1990*

NB: For the meaning of "Secretary of State", see page 24.

Whilst the laws for the protection of the environment are for the most part found in statutes, the strength of the common law must not be overlooked. Over the centuries the common law has been a powerful weapon against those who do harm by contaminating air, earth or water. This chapter describes the law of nuisance as a valuable tool for conservation, and the statute laws which provide weapons against nuisances, controls over hazards and regulation of waste disposal.

1. Nuisance

The law of nuisance gives a remedy to owners and occupiers when the use or enjoyment of land is unlawfully interfered with by such violations as excessive smells, noise, vibration, or by pollution in any form. It also gives redress when the public at large suffers such annoyances. A nuisance at law is simply what the name suggests, the committing of a substantial nuisance to others. It may be a private or public nuisance at common law, or a statutory nuisance. One of the merits of the law is that it offers legal process to halt continuing or threatened nuisances, as well as recompense to injured parties.

(a) Public nuisance

A public nuisance is an unlawful interference with public rights, or with the comfort or convenience of the public at large, or a section of the public. For example, the carrying on of noisy or noisome trades or building operations may be a public nuisance if it is too much of an annoyance to the public. An individual person or body suffering damage beyond that suffered by the public in general may take proceedings, as for example when an obstruction to the highway blocks access to an individual's business premises causing him loss. It is open to the Attorney-General to take proceedings in the civil courts to stop nuisances on behalf of the public, either on his own initiative, or (in the legal phrase) "on the relation of" others who may be joined as plaintiffs with him.

(b) Private nuisance

Lord Wright in *Sedleigh-Denfield* v *O'Callaghan* [1940] AC 880 (HL) said that a private nuisance is an unlawful interference with a person's use or enjoyment of property or some right over, or in connection with it. It is a tort—a wrong for which people may sue in a civil (not a criminal) court. It is a law of common sense and reasonableness, striking a balance between the right of persons to use their property for lawful purposes and the right of neighbours not to have the enjoyment of their property spoilt by others, Lord Wright went on to explain. The criterion for a right of legal action is whether an ordinary right-thinking person— in the phrase beloved of judges, "the man on the Clapham omnibus"— would consider the nuisance unreasonable. Where physical damage is done by the nuisance—for example, noxious fumes which damage a neighbour's trees as in *St Helens Smelting Co* v *Tipping* (1865) 11 HLC 642—the unreasonableness speaks for itself. Where no physical damage is done, account must be taken of such matters as the degree of the nuisance, the timing of the interference and the nature of the locality. People must expect farming to be carried out in the countryside with the smells and noises from farm operations and livestock. But a manure heap placed so close to a neighbour's house as to be "a serious inconvenience and interference with the comfort of the occupiers" was an unreasonable nuisance (*Bland* v *Yates* (1914) 58 Sol Jo 612) and so was an excessive number of cockerels crowing early in the morning in a rural residential area (*Leeman* v *Montagu* [1936] 2 All ER 677).

(c) Remedies

What is reasonable or unreasonable is not always easy to assess, but where a nuisance is unreasonable the injured party can claim damages and an injunction.

An injunction is an order to stop the nuisance. It is a contempt of court to disobey an injunction, for which the wrongdoer may be committed to prison or receive other condign punishment. An injunction can therefore be an effective shield against activities harming or threatening the environment, especially emissions from industrial premises such as poisonous fumes, effluents or airborne particles. An injunction is not automatically given on proving an actionable nuisance, as it is a discretionary remedy. It will not be issued if damages are a sufficient remedy, or if the court considers an injunction inappropriate, for example, where it will cause hardship out of proportion to the harm done, or where the nuisance is temporary. Sometimes, however, an injunction will be granted pending the hearing of the case until the issues can be fully examined at the trial.

The law permits the injured party to abate a nuisance, but it is a remedy to be exercised with the utmost caution. As it is unlikely to be appropriate where a nuisance significantly harms the environment, the bounds of self-help are not examined here. It is enough to say that it is only too easy for the person injured to put a foot wrong in tackling the nuisance and to be converted from an innocent party to a wrongdoer.

(d) Strict liability for escapes: Rylands v Fletcher

A handy adjunct of the law of nuisance is known as "the rule in *Rylands* v *Fletcher*" (1868) LR 3 HL 330. The rule is quoted on p 83 below. It is a rule of strict liability for anything kept on land "likely to do mischief if it escapes". If it does escape there is liability for all the damage it causes, unless the escape was due to an act of God, the claimant's own fault, or the action of a third party over whom the defendant had no control. In *Rylands* v *Fletcher* mine water escaped, but the rule has been applied to a wide variety of substances, including colliery spoil (*Attorney-General* v *Cory Bros* [1921] 1 AC 521); sewage (*Humphries* v *Cousins* (1877) 2 CPD 239); acid smuts (*Halsey* v *Esso* [1961] 1 WLR 683); paraffin (*Mulholland & Tedd Ltd* v *Baker* [1939] 3 All ER 253); cricket balls hit for six (*Miller* v *Jackson* [1977] 3 WLR 20); and even to gypsies (*Attorney-General* v *Corke* [1939] Ch 89). The courts used to hold that the rule did not apply to anything naturally on the land, but since the case of the land slip at Barrow Mump (*Leakey* v *National Trust* [1980] 1 All ER 17) it is evidently no longer so.

(e) Defence of "statutory authority"

A less satisfactory rule, which has often worked unfairly, is that where duties are required to be carried out by statute, and in doing so damage is caused to others, or to the public in general, the body performing them is not liable in nuisance or under *Rylands* v *Fletcher*. It means that negligence must be proved if a legal remedy is to be obtained. Statutory bodies have therefore escaped liability for escapes of sewage (*Smeaton* v *Ilford Corporation* [1954] Ch 450), gas (*Dunne* v *North Western Gas Board* [1964] 2 QB 806) and other harmful substances.

2. Statutory nuisance

The nuisance laws considered above enable claims to be made at common law for damages and injunctions. They are backed up by more precise laws of statutory nuisance with criminal penalties attached. The laws of statutory nuisance have been conveniently brought together from previous Public Health Acts and other legislation in the Environmental Protection Act 1990 ("EPA 1990"). The Act specifies what are statutory nuisances (s 79), and provides a system for local authorities to serve abatement notices and for magistrates' courts to make abatement orders. The full provisions are in Part III of the EPA 1990 and Schedule 3. They are summarised here so far as they are important for conservation.

Every local authority has a duty "to cause its area to be inspected from time to time to detect any statutory nuisances", and to investigate any complaint made by any person living within its area (s 79(1)).

(a) What are statutory nuisances?

If they are "prejudicial to health or a nuisance" the following are statutory nuisances—smoke, fumes, gases or noise emitted from premises; dust, steam, smells or other effluvia arising on industrial, trade or business premises; and accumulations and deposits. Premises kept in such a state, or animals kept in such a place or manner, as to be prejudicial to health or a nuisance, are also statutory nuisances together with anything declared to be so by other legislation (EPA 1990, s 79(1)).

As ever, there are exceptions and qualifications (set out in s 79(3), (4), (5) and (6)) that practitioners may need to study in detail, as regards emissions of fumes and gases, smoke and "dark smoke", steam and smoke from railway locomotives and noise caused by aircraft other than model aircraft. There are exemptions for Crown and Ministry of Defence premises occupied for naval, military or airforce purposes, or by visiting forces (s 79(2)). A number of terms are defined in section 79(7), such as "dust", "fumes", "noise", "smoke" and "dark smoke". Separate legislation on clean air and noise is dealt with below.

(b) Abatement notices

Where a local authority is satisfied that a statutory nuisance exists, or is likely to occur or recur in its area, it shall serve an abatement notice requiring its abatement and/or prohibiting or restricting its occurrence or recurrence. The notice may require works to be done or other steps taken. It must specify a time limit for complying with the notice (s 80(1)). The notice is served on the person responsible for the nuisance, or where appropriate the owner or occupier of the premises (s 80(2)). The person served may appeal to a magistrates' court within 21 days (s 80(3)).

Failure to comply with any requirement of an abatement notice without reasonable excuse is an offence for which the offender may be fined. An additional fine may be imposed for each day the offence continues (s 80(5)). A heavier fine (present maximum £20,000) may be imposed where the offence is on industrial, trade or business premises (s 80(6)). Where there is failure to comply with a notice, the local authority has the right to abate the nuisance itself and recover the reasonable cost from the offender (s 81(3), (4)). If a local authority considers the remedies available in the magistrates' court inadequate, it may proceed against an offender in the High Court "for the purpose of securing the abatement, prohibition or restriction of the nuisance" (s 81(5)).

Further details of procedures, and the powers of entry of a local authority, are in Schedule 3.

(c) Abatement orders

The statutory nuisance laws are not just for local authorities. It is open to any person aggrieved by a statutory nuisance to seek an abatement order from the magistrates' court under section 82 of the 1990 Act. The court can make an order with similar directions to a local authority abatement notice, and can impose a fine there and then (s 82(2)), and order compensation to be paid to the complainant for any expenses properly incurred in bringing proceedings (s 82(12)). Before taking proceedings the complainant must give the offender notice in writing of his intention to do so (s 82(6)), but does not need to serve an abatement notice (*Sandwell MBC* v *Bujok* [1990] 1 WLR 1350 (HL)). In the case of noise nuisance, at least three days' notice must be given. In other cases, at least 21 days' notice (s 82(7)). Failure to comply with an abatement order is an offence for which a fine may be imposed (s 82(8)).

(d) Defence of "best practical means"

In certain circumstances it is a defence to a charge of failing to comply with an abatement notice or abatement order, to show that "the best practical means" were used to prevent or to counteract the effects of the nuisance (ss 80(7) and 82(9)). Whether the defence is available depends on the nature of the nuisance, the kind of premises and, in some instances, whether offending smoke was emitted from a chimney. The permutations can be found in sections 79(9), 80(8) and 82(9)).

3. Integrated pollution control and local authority air pollution control

Statutory water pollution control has been a feature of English law for over a century. It is now a duty of the National Rivers Authority and is dealt with in Chapter 6. Other kinds of pollution control have gradually accumulated. Part I of the EPA 1990 introduced two new systems, namely integrated pollution control and local authority air pollution control. They take the place of some of the previous controls under various Acts (but not those of the National Rivers Authority). How long the systems will remain in their present form has been thrown into question by the proposal for a new environmental agency bringing together all the functions of the National Rivers Authority, Her Majesty's Inspectorate of Pollution ("HMIP") and the waste regulation work of local authorities.

Integrated pollution control is carried out by "the chief inspector appointed for England and Wales by the Secretary of State", the statutory guise of HMIP, and to some extent by the Secretary of State for the Environment. It is for the control of industrial processes which have a significant potential for pollution. Local authorities are given control over emissions to air from some less polluting processes. It is convenient to take the two systems together as the EPA 1990 does. The HMIP is the result of a merger of the Inspectorates for Radiochemical and Hazardous Waste and for Industrial Air Pollution. It is presently part of the Department of the Environment.

(a) "Enforcing authorities"

The HMIP and the relevant local authorities are called the "enforcing authorities".

(b) Control systems

Regulations made by the Secretary of State determine the details of who controls what and to some extent how. The Secretary of State prescribes by statutory instrument the processes subject to central control by HMIP or to local control by local authorities, and prescribes substances the release of which into the environment is subject to central or local control. The Environmental Protection (Prescribed Processes and Substances) Regulations 1991, SI 1991 No 472 (amended by SI 1991 No 836 and SI 1992 No 614), sets out many pages of prescribed processes under the headings of Production of Fuel and Power; Iron and Steel; Mineral Industries; Chemical Industry; Waste Disposal and Recycling; and "Other Industries". It then sets out lists of substances prescribed for (1) release into the air (for example, halogens, oxides of sulphur, phosphorus and particulate matter); (2) release into water (for example mercury, cadmium, aldrin, endrin and dieldrin); and (3) release into land (for example, organic solvents, azides, phosphorus and pesticides).

Control is by requiring authorisation from the enforcing authority for carrying on prescribed processes (s 6) and by implying by law, in every authorisation, a condition that the person carrying on the process must "use the best available techniques not entailing excessive cost":

(i)   "for preventing the release of substances prescribed for any environmental medium into that medium"; or where that is impracticable, for reducing the release to a minimum and for rendering it harmless; and

(ii)   for rendering harmless any other substances which might cause harm if released into any environmental medium (s 7(4)).

Further explanation of what the techniques include can be found in section 7(10).

The 1990 Act enables the Secretary of State to make regulations "establishing standards, objectives or requirements in relation to particular prescribed processes or particular substances", and to set standard limits to releases and standard requirements for the measurement or analysis of releases, and standard quality objectives and quality standards for substances. He may also "make plans", under a notice procedure, establishing limits for the total amount of any substances to be released into the UK environment, and allocate quotas, so as progressively to reduce pollution of the environment (s 3).

Practitioners may need to refer to the many definitions of terms in section 1 of the EPA 1990, and to the statutory objectives for attaching conditions to authorisations in section 7.

(c) Authorisations

It is illegal for any person to carry on a prescribed process except under an authorisation granted by the enforcing authority and in accordance with its conditions, including the implied "best available technique" condition noted above. Procedures, and the conditions and content of authorisations, are dealt with in sections 6–12 and Schedule 1 of the 1990 Act. Transfers (s 9), variation (ss 10 and 11) and revocation (s 12) of authorisations are provided for. An important safeguard is that "any person" may make representations regarding applications for the grant or variation of an authorisation (Sch 1 paras 2(5) and 6(6)). The Secretary of State has power to give directions to the HMIP and local authorities regarding any application for an authorisation and conditions to be included in it, may give guidance (s 7(11)) and may call in any application for his own determination (Sch 1 para 3). Fees may be charged for applying for an authorisation or a variation of one, and for holding an authorisation (s 8).

(d) Enforcement

Inspectors of HMIP and local authorities are given wide powers to enter premises, inspect, examine, take measurements and photographs, make recordings, take possession or samples of articles or substances, require questions to be answered and records to be produced and to take other investigative and precautionary actions (s 17). An inspector finding an article or substance that he reasonably believes is a cause of imminent danger or serious harm, may seize it and render it harmless (s 18).

Enforcing authorities may serve enforcement notices specifying steps to be taken where they are of opinion that an authorisation is being, or is likely to be, contravened (s 13). They may serve prohibition notices specifying steps to be taken where they are of opinion that the continuing of a prescribed process under an authorisation, or the continuing of it in a particular manner, "involves an imminent risk of serious pollution of the environment". The notice will direct steps to be taken to remove the risk and direct that the authorisation, wholly or to a stated extent, shall cease to have effect (s 14). The Secretary of State may give directions whether or not to serve enforcement and prohibition notices, and may make directions about the content of the notices (ss 13(3) and 14(4)).

(e) Offences

Section 23 of the 1990 Act creates a range of offences for such things as carrying on a prescribed process without authorisation, contravening the terms of an authorisation, or an enforcement notice or prohibition notice, obstructing an inspector in the performance of his duties, making false or misleading statements to obtain an authorisation, or when otherwise required to give information under the Act, forging documents, falsifying records and pretending to be an inspector. For the more serious offences the maximum fine is £20,000 on summary conviction, but for any of the offences on indictment an unlimited fine and/or imprisonment up to two years may be imposed.

By section 27, the HMIP is given power, where certain offences are committed causing harm, to remedy the harm and recover the reasonable expense from anyone convicted of the offence. The written approval of the Secretary of State is required before exercising this power, and no steps may be taken on, or affecting land, where no prescribed process is being carried on, without the consent of the occupier.

(f) Appeals

Provision is made for appeals to the Secretary of State against the refusal of authorisations, or conditions attached to them, and against variation or revocation of them (s 15).

(g) Public registers

Any person may object to the grant of an authorisation or its variation (Sch 1 paras 2(5) and 6(6)). So that relevant information is available to the public, every enforcing authority must keep a register of applications, authorisations, variation notices, enforcement notices, prohibition notices, revocations, appeals, convictions of offences, directions from the Secretary of State and sundry other facts (s 20). Registers must be available for public inspection at all reasonable times free of charge (s 20(7)). Information affecting national security is not to be included on public registers (s 21), nor commercially confidential information (s 22) unless it is of a description that the Secretary of State has directed must be included in the public interest (s 22(7)).

4. Other clean air legislation

(a) Smoke

The Clean Air Act 1956 was revolutionary in transforming the quality of air and the cleanliness of city buildings. The author recalls, as an RAF navigator in the 1940s, how London was always seen from the air with a purple pall of smoke overhanging it. The opaque fogs and "smogs", common in those times, are unknown to the present generation. They have been banished by the implementation of the Clean Air Acts and regulations made under them.

The Clean Air Act 1993 consolidated into one statute the Clean Air

Acts 1956–1968, Part IV of the Control of Pollution Act 1974 and several other bits and pieces of clean air legislation, with only minor amendments. It came into force on 27 August 1993. The original provisions are now repealed. A total job of consolidation was not done, as the clean air provisions in Parts I and III of the EPA 1990 remain in the 1990 Act. The Clean Air Act 1993, s 41, expressly states Parts I and III of the 1993 Act shall not apply to any prescribed processes under the EPA 1990. As Part II (dealing with smoke, grit, dust and fumes) does apply to the EPA processes, there appears to be scope for confusion regarding the responsibilities of local authorities.

Re-enacting provisions originally in the 1956 Act, the Clean Air Act 1993, among other things, makes it an offence to emit (subject to exceptions) "dark smoke" from chimneys (Part I); regulates the installation of new furnaces, requires new furnaces above a given size to be designed to prevent the emission of grit and dust as far as practicable, and gives local authorities duties regarding the approval of furnace designs (Part II); enables local authorities to designate smoke control areas, and to give grants to adapt domestic fireplaces to burn smokeless fuels, gives powers to ministers to make regulations, including regulations specifying fuels authorised to be used in smoke control areas, and prohibits retailers from delivering unauthorised fuels to buildings in smoke control areas (Part III).

The Act re-enacts the provisions originally in the 1968 Act prohibiting the emission of dark smoke from industrial or trade premises, otherwise than from a chimney—for example, from fires in the open (s 2). Domestic bonfires, however, are not banned.

"Dark smoke" is smoke as dark as, or darker than, Shade 2 on what is known as a Ringelmann Chart. The test has to be carried out in a proper fashion to get a true comparison.

(b) Straw and stubble burning

The most efficient and economical way for farmers to clear fields of stubble and straw, especially in the absence of a market or local use for straw, has been to burn it off. The public and neighbours frequently complained about smoke from burning fields in the late summer, and at times irresponsible burning caused dangers and damage. In attempts to reduce or eliminate the nuisance and danger, the National Farmers' Union issued a Code of Practice and some local authorities made bye-laws to tackle the problem, but the continuation of the nuisance led to primary legislation in the EPA 1990.

By section 152 of the 1990 Act the Minister of Agriculture, Fisheries and Food and the Secretary of State are empowered to make regulations to prohibit or restrict the burning of crop residues (defined as "straw or stubble or any other crop residue") on agricultural land by persons engaged in agriculture. Regulations may include exceptions as regards particular localities, crop residues and circumstances, and they may create offences and may repeal existing byelaws. By the Crop Residues (Burning)

Regulations 1993 (SI 1993 No 1366) it is an offence to burn on agricultural land cereal straw, cereal stubble and the residues of oil-seed rape, field beans harvested dry and peas harvested dry. Exceptions allow such burning, subject to specified safeguards, for the purposes of education and research, or disease or pest control, or disposal of the remains of straw stacks or broken bales. An order repealing local authority byelaws (Burning of Crop Residues (Repeal of Byelaws) Order 1992, SI 1992 No 693) came into effect on 2 April 1992. The power to make byelaws in section 43 of the Criminal Justice Act 1982 was terminated by EPA 1990, Sch 15 para 21.

(c) Heather and grass burning

The burning of heather and grass is also controlled. The Heather and Grass (Burning) Regulations 1986 (SI 1986 No 428) allow burning between 1 October and the following 15 April in the uplands, and between 1 November and 31 March in the lowlands. Otherwise a licence is needed from the Ministry of Agriculture, Fisheries and Food or the Welsh Office, who have a code of guidance on the subject.

(d) Gases and Vapours

In addition to the provisions of Part I of the EPA 1990, described above, section 85 of the Act adds a new section 7A to the Clean Air Act 1968, applying some sections of the Clean Air Act 1956 to "prescribed gases". The sections applied are those dealing with grit and dust, and the requirement that new furnaces should, as far as practicable, be smokeless. They must now also be gasless. The provision is now in the Clean Air Act 1993. The gases concerned are prescribed in regulations, and may include vapour and moisture precipitated from vapour.

5. Noise

Intrusive noise merits legislation of its own and gets it in Part III of the Control of Pollution Act 1974 ("COPA 1974"). A weakness of the law is that one of the worst forms of pollution and nuisance affecting the quality of life of vast numbers of people, namely aircraft noise, is excluded from the anti-noise legislation, and common law claims are virtually impossible because of evidential difficulties and the high degree of protection against claims in the Air Navigation Acts.

Rural noise nuisance can usually and best be dealt with under the statutory nuisance laws (above). "Noise" in both COPA 1974 and EPA 1990 includes vibration. COPA 1974 is useful for controlling noise from industrial and construction sites, rather than the countryside. It is therefore described here in summary only. Practitioners should note that sections 57(a), 58 and 59 of COPA 1974 have been repealed, with consequential deletions following, by EPA 1990.

By section 63 of the COPA 1974, a local authority has power to make noise abatement orders designating some or all of its area as a noise abatement zone. Every local authority has a duty to inspect its area from time to time to decide how to exercise this power (s 57(b)). An order requires confirmation by the Secretary of State. A noise level register is kept for certain classes of premises in a noise abatement zone which must not be exceeded without the local authority's consent in writing. The register must be open to public inspection free of charge at all reasonable hours (s 63(7)). A contravention of a registered noise level, or of a condition of a consent, is an offence for which a fine may be imposed (ss 65(5) and 74).

After a conviction a magistrates' court may order the execution of works to prevent the excessive noise continuing or recurring, and contravention of the order is a further offence. The court may instead, or in addition, direct the local authority to do it (s 65(6), (7)).

The local authority has a general power to serve a notice on the person responsible for any premises to which a noise abatement order applies, requiring him to reduce the noise emanating from the premises, to prevent its recurrence and to take specified steps to achieve it. Contravention of the notice without reasonable excuse is an offence (s 66).

The COPA 1974 also gives a local authority powers to control the noise from construction sites (ss 60 and 61). The Secretary of State can make regulations limiting the noise of plant and machinery (s 68). Subject to exceptions, it is an offence to operate a loudspeaker in a street between 9 pm and 8 am (s 62).

6. Hazardous substances control

The laws and procedures concerning hazardous substances, formerly in the Housing and Planning Act 1986, are now in the Planning (Hazardous Substances) Act 1990 and regulations made under both Acts. As with so much modern legislation, the law is drafted in a complex fashion. The section references in the following paragraphs are to the Planning (Hazardous Substances) Act 1990 unless otherwise indicated.

The presence of a "hazardous substance" (so designated by regulations) on, over or under land requires a "hazardous substances consent" from the hazardous substances authority, unless the quantity of it is less than the prescribed level for the substance. The hazardous substances authority is usually the local planning authority (s 1), but it is the county council in respect of national parks (except where there is a joint planning board), or in respect of mineral-working land or land used for refuse or waste disposal (s 3). It is the Broads Authority in the Broads (s 3(3)), and it is the appropriate Minister where the land is operational land of statutory undertakers (s 2).

Regulations specify a "controlled quantity" for each substance prescribed as hazardous. No consent is required for the presence of less than the controlled quantity in, on or under the land, together with any land or structure within 500m controlled by the same person (s 4(2)). When a consent is given (or is deemed), it enures for the benefit of the land

and all persons for the time being holding an interest in the land (s 6). Consent is deemed where a substance was present within 12 months preceding the date on which the Act came into force (August 1990). Consents may be given subject to conditions and may be varied and revoked. If they are varied or revoked, compensation may be claimed by persons suffering damage in consequence of it (s 16). An important provision allows the Secretary of State to call in an application for consent for his own decision (s 20).

Section 23 sets out a series of offences for various contraventions of hazardous substances control, for which the penalty is a fine. It is a defence to these offences for the accused to show that he took all reasonable precautions and exercised all due diligence to avoid the offence, or that the offence could only be avoided by breach of a statutory duty. It is also a defence to show that the accused did not know and had no reason to believe that the hazardous substance was present, or that it exceeded the controlled quantity or the amount for which consent was given.

(a) Radioactive substances

Generally the EPA 1990 and the Planning (Hazardous Substances) Act 1990 do not apply to radioactive waste for which control by central government is provided by the Radioactive Substances Act 1993, the Nuclear Installations Acts 1965 and 1969, and regulations. Radioactive material may only be kept or used by authorised and registered undertakings and may only be disposed of as authorised. Nuclear installations are subject to site licensing by the Health and Safety Executive under the 1965 Act. Section 7 imposes a duty on the licensee of a nuclear site to secure that no ionising radiations emitted from any waste from the site, cause damage to any property or person.

However, in *Merlin v British Nuclear Fuels plc* [1990] 3 WLR 383, where a family sold up and moved because their house became contaminated by radionuclides, Gatehouse J refused their claim, saying "damage" in the Act meant physical damage. They could not claim for the economic loss caused to them.

The Radioactive Substances Act 1993 came into force on 17 August 1993. It consolidated much of the previous legislation on the subject, which is now repealed.

(b) Some other hazards legislation

From the mass of other legislation and regulations, the following miscellany is noted to indicate the range. The EPA 1990, s 140 gives wide powers to the Secretary of State to prohibit or restrict the importation, use, supply and storage of any substance or article which might pollute the environment or cause harm to the health of humans, animals or plants.

Important regulations are made under the Health and Safety at Work

Act 1974 (especially SI 1988 No 1657). Regulations control the conveyance of dangerous substances by road (especially SI 1981 No 1059 and 1986 No 1951), and the carriage of explosives (1989 No 615). There are regulations for classifying, packaging and labelling dangerous substances (SI 1984 No 1244); and regulations governing highly flammable liquids and gases (SI 1972 No 917). Regulations are also made under the Farm and Garden Chemicals Act 1967.

7. Waste regulation and disposal

Our "throw-away" society generates vast amounts of domestic, commercial and industrial waste. In the South East Waste Regulation counties alone, including London, 32,017,903 tonnes of waste were deposited in 1992. It has to be planned for, collected, treated and disposed of somehow. Present legislation places the responsibility on local authorities. It is planned, however, that the promised new Environmental Agency will assume this responsibility, but at the time of writing no proposals for the new regime have been disclosed, if they have been decided upon. In view of what may be imminent dismantling of the present system, and the breadth of the subject, present arrangements are no more than sketched in here.

The legislation governing waste regulation and disposal is found in Part II of EPA 1990, which replaces and strengthens laws formerly in COPA 1974. The deposit of waste on land generally requires planning permission (Town and Country Planning Act 1990, s 53(3)), and planning of waste disposal by planning authorities is mandatory (s 38, as substituted by Planning and Compensation Act 1991, Sch 4). The Mines and Quarries (Tips) Act 1969 is designed to see that disused tips are made secure and do not constitute a danger. The Control of Pollution (Amendment) Act 1989 requires registration of waste carriers and has provisions against "fly tipping".

The local authorities concerned with waste are waste regulation authorities, waste collection authorities and waste disposal authorities. By section 30 of the EPA 1990, in non-metropolitan counties the county councils are both the waste regulation and waste disposal authorities. Specific waste regulation authorities have been created for most metropolitan areas. Outside Greater London the waste collection authorities are the district councils, and within Greater London they are generally the borough councils. The waste disposal authorities in the metropolitan counties and London are as variously set out in section 30(2). Where an authority is both a waste regulation and a waste disposal authority, it must keep its regulation and disposal functions separate (s 30(7)).

(a) Waste regulation

The functions of waste regulation authorities cover, among other things—

(i) investigating what arrangements are needed for treating and disposing of household, industrial and commercial waste (known to the Act as "controlled waste", s 75(4)), and preparing waste disposal plans (s 50);

(ii)   issuing and administering waste disposal licences (ss 35–41);

(iii) ensuring that disposal activities or accumulations of waste do not cause pollution of the environment or harm to human health (ss 42 and 61);

(iv) dealing with contraventions (s 59);

(v)   maintaining a public register of licences, applications, notices, convictions and other information (s 64);

(vi) appointing inspectors (s 68).

(b) Waste collection

The function of waste collection authorities is, among other things, to collect household waste in their areas free of charge, and, if requested by the occupier of premises, commercial waste for a fee (s 45), and to deliver the waste for disposal as directed by the waste disposal authority (s 48).

(c) Waste disposal

The functions of waste disposal authorities are, among other things, to arrange for—

(i)   the disposal by contractors of waste collected in their areas (s 51);

(ii)   civic amenity sites for residents in their areas to deposit household waste (s 51);

(iii) recycling of waste and paying recycling credits (ss 55 and 82).

(d) Offences

Section 33(1) of the EPA 1990 lays down these offences—

(i)   to deposit controlled waste, or knowingly cause or permit it to be deposited, in or on any land, unless a waste management licence authorising it is held and the deposit is in accordance with the licence;

(ii)   to treat, keep or dispose of controlled waste, or knowingly cause or permit it, except under and in accordance with a waste management licence;

(iii) to treat, keep or dispose of controlled waste in a manner likely to cause pollution of the environment or harm to human health.

These offences are not committed as respects household waste from domestic property, which is treated, kept or disposed of within the curtilage of the dwellinghouse by, or with the permission of, the occupier (s 33(2)). There are also defences of taking all reasonable precautions; due diligence; acting under an employer's instructions; and emergency action (set out in s 33(7)).

The Divisional Court has held that seaweed is not "controlled waste", and therefore it is not an offence to deposit it on land without a licence (*Thanet DC* v *Kent CC,* The Times, 15 March 1993).

Practitioners will need to see the many definitions of terms in section 29.

8. Litter

Leaving litter in town or country is a besetting sin of the public. The original Litter Act of 1958 was a failure. It simply was not enforced. Current legislation, in Part IV of the EPA 1990, recognises the need to do more than bring occasional prosecutions. It imposes duties on authorities and occupiers to keep highways and certain lands free of litter, and gives the public a hand in enforcing the law.

(a) The basic offence

Section 87(1) of the EPA 1990 provides:

> "If any person throws down, drops or otherwise deposits in, into or from any place to which this section applies, and leaves, any thing whatsoever in such circumstances as to cause, or contribute to, or tend to lead to, the defacement by litter of any place to which this section applies, he shall, subject to subsection (2) below, be guilty of an offence".

This is reasonably comprehensible until the meaning of "any place to which this section applies" is sought. It requires an examination of section 87(3) and (4) along with pages of wordy definitions in section 86 and further definitions in section 98, which practitioners will study when necessary. It is enough here to state that the offence is committed when the offending act is done (1) in a place in the open air to which the public are entitled or permitted to have access without payment (any covered place open to the air on at least one side counts); and (2) in certain other places open to the air on at least one side to which the public can go with or without payment. These other places include most highways, and certain lands controlled by local authorities, the Crown, government departments, and certain other statutory bodies, education bodies, and land within a "litter control area". "Litter control areas" may be designated by certain local authorities. It may only include land, of a description laid down in orders of the Secretary of State, which in their opinion would be detrimental to the amenities of the locality if litter or refuse were present (s 90).

The section 87(1) offence is not committed if the depositing and leaving is authorised by law, or is done with the consent of the owner, occupier or person or authority having control of the place.

(b) Fixed penalty

A "litter authority" (local authorities, national park authorities and the Broads Authority (s 88(9))) believing a section 87 offence has been committed may serve a notice on the supposed offender offering the opportunity of paying a fixed penalty within 14 days. If he pays it within that time he cannot be convicted of the offence. The fixed penalty is currently £10. The Secretary of State may change it by order (s 88).

(c) Duty to keep land and highways litter free

A key piece in the jigsaw of litter law is the duty imposed by section 89 of the 1990 Act on sundry authorities and bodies, and occupiers of lands in litter control areas, to ensure that "relevant land" under their control is, so far as practicable, kept clear of litter and refuse, and that highways and roads they are responsible for are kept clean. "Relevant land" is land so designated by the local authority to which the public are entitled to have access (s 86(12)).

(d) Litter abatement orders

Section 91 of the 1990 Act allows a complaint to be made to a magistrates' court "by any person on the ground that he is aggrieved by the defacement by litter or refuse" of sundry kinds of places listed in the section. These places are in the main highways, roads and lands on which it is an offence to commit the basic litter offence quoted above. A complaint can also be made on the ground of want of cleanliness of certain highways and roads. The proceedings are brought against the person who has a duty under section 89(1) or (2) to keep the land clear or the highway clean as noted in the preceding paragraph. A "principal litter authority" cannot make a complaint under this section. If satisfied that the complaint is made out, the court can make a litter abatement order, and may order the defendant to pay the reasonable expenses of the complainant in bringing the proceedings. Failure to comply with the terms of a litter abatement order is an offence (s 91(9)).

(e) Notice procedures by principal litter authorities

Principal litter authorities can tackle the leaving of litter by way of "litter abatement notices" (s 92), under procedures akin to nuisance abatement notices, and they have power to issue "street litter control notices" on occupiers of premises imposing requirements with a view to the prevention of accumulation of litter or refuse in and around any street or open land adjacent to any street (ss 93 and 94).

(f) Litter on wheels

The unresolved problem of abandoned vehicles disfiguring the countryside can be tackled under the Refuse Disposal (Amenity) Act 1978. It is an offence under the Act to abandon a vehicle without lawful authority on any land in the open air (s 2), and district councils have a duty to remove them (s 3) and may recover the cost from the owners, if they were aware of the abandonment, or from the persons abandoning them. The 1990 Act gives local authorities the power, under a procedure set out in section 99 and Schedule 4, to seize and dispose of abandoned shopping and luggage trolleys.

9. Pesticides

Controls over pesticides in Part III of the Food and Environment Protection Act 1985 are outlined in Chapter 7. The object of the legislation is not simply to protect wildlife. It aims also to safeguard human health and to eliminate unwanted consequences from pesticides. Powers are given to Ministers to seize pesticides imported, supplied, stored or used illegally, and to dispose of them together with any crops or other things treated with them.

(a) Crop spraying

Crop spraying from aircraft is regulated by the Air Navigation Order 1989 (SI 1989 No 2004), art 45. Only operators holding an aerial application certificate for the purpose, from the Civil Aviation Authority, may undertake spraying from the air, and only after notifying certain authorities and undertakers and landowners and occupiers in the vicinity.

10. Genetically modified organisms

Genetic engineering can produce wonders, said to be beneficial, by way, for example, of generating plant strains immune to diseases, rapid food, and new pharmaceutical products and processes of various kinds, but genetically modified organisms ("GMOs") outside controlled conditions may have dangers. Part VI of the EPA 1990 (amended by SI 1992 No 2617 to give effect to EC Directive 90/220 on the deliberate release of GMOs into the environment) therefore "has effect for the purpose of preventing or minimising any damage to the environment which may arise from the escape or release from human control of genetically modified organisms" (s 106(1)).

The definitions in the Act are less simple, but *Which* magazine of March 1992 tells us succinctly that GMOs are "plants, animals or microbes whose genes have been altered in a laboratory to achieve certain characteristics".

In brief, the 1990 Act requires (subject to exceptions) any person who imports, acquires, releases or markets any GMO to assess the risk of damage to the environment in so doing. Before doing any of those things he must notify the Secretary of State of his intention, furnishing prescribed information (s 108). Where there appears to be a risk, he shall not carry out the risky activity, he must keep under control any GMOs he has, and, where necessary, "shall use the best available techniques not entailing excessive cost" for preventing damage to the environment (s 109). The Secretary of State may serve prohibition notices forbidding any person from importing, acquiring, releasing or marketing any GMO (s 110), and (inevitably subject to exceptions) none of these things may be done without a consent granted by the Secretary of State (ss 111 and 112). Inspectors have rights to enter and inspect premises (s 115), and the Act creates a series of offences for contraventions and other wrongdoings in connection with the GMO laws (s 118).

Chapter 5

Protection of land

Abbreviations in this chapter:

TCPA 1990 = *Town and Country Planning Act 1990*
EA = *Environmental assessment*
GDO = *General development order*
TPO = *Tree preservation order*

NB: For the meaning of "Secretary of State", see page 24.

In a book of this kind, overlapping is bound to occur between chapters. Every chapter concerns land. Land at law includes buildings and at least the bed and banks of rivers, lakes and canals. They are the subject of Chapters 8 and 6. The designations in Chapter 3 are designations of land, and the laws against nuisance and dangers described in Chapter 4 are largely protective of land. This chapter therefore picks up terrestrial subjects not dealt with elsewhere and deals with the town and country planning system.

A. The planning system

The planning laws are a conservation tool. They are a severe restraint on the right of owners and occupiers to use their land as they will. The original Town and Country Planning Act of 1947, setting the mould for the current system, was a hefty enough volume. Since then planning law has constantly expanded until a massive body of primary and subordinate legislation has accumulated. The Town and Country Planning Act 1990 alone has 337 sections and 17 schedules. An outline is sketched here to give background understanding and some useful references. Numerous textbooks are available if and when a full treatment is needed.

1. The main legislation

Fortunately the primary legislation was collected into three reasonably orderly, though complex, Acts in 1990, with a fourth taking care of consequential and temporary matters arising from the consolidation. The three Acts are the Town and Country Planning Act 1990 ("TCPA 1990"), the Planning (Listed Buildings and Conservation Areas) Act 1990 and the Planning (Hazardous Substances) Act 1990. These repealed and re-enacted existing Acts with only minor changes and were accompanied by the Planning (Consequential Provisions) Act 1990. This useful consolidation had hardly reached the statute book when the Planning and Compensation Act 1991 made substantial additions and amendments to the Acts.

The subordinate legislation (regulations and orders, mostly in statutory instruments) which had been made under the Acts that were repealed in 1990, continued in force. More has been generated since.

The Acts have separate Parts for England and Wales on the one hand, and Scotland on the other, and there are some miscellaneous provisions applying to both. This chapter deals only with the law for England and Wales.

2. Control of development

The planning system is about the control of development. Planning control is an executive function of local authorities, presided over by the Secretary of State for the Environment. He exercises influence over planning policies by issuing guidance to planning authorities in circulars and, more lately, Planning Policy Guidance Notes. He also has numerous powers in the planning process. He can call in planning applications for his own decision. He decides appeals from refusals of planning authorities to grant planning permissions, and other decisions of theirs. He makes orders, such as the important general development orders (GDOs). He gives directions. Structure plans require his approval, and he, of course, initiates planning legislation.

Planning powers over rural land are apportioned between county councils and district councils, with some overlap. The Secretary of State can appoint joint planning boards for two or more counties or districts, if he thinks it expedient to do so (TCPA 1990, s 2).

In metropolitan districts the metropolitan district council is the planning authority, and in London the borough councils. The Secretary of State can confer planning powers on urban development corporations where he thinks fit.

Control is exercised by giving or refusing permission where applications are made for permission to carry out such development as is subject to planning control. Planning is therefore negative to a large degree. Planners can say "Thou shalt not", but cannot say "Thou shalt", undertake development. A positive element is instilled, however, by the preparation of plans and policies against which planning applications are decided.

In simple terms, county council control is strategic, district control is tactical, with county councils setting out the broad strategy for the amount and general locality of development and land uses of different kinds in their counties, and the district councils setting out the planning policies with greater particularity for areas within their districts. County council planning strategy covers, among other things, housing policy, highways, mineral extraction, waste disposal and green belts. Applications for development permission are made to the district councils. They decide whether to grant or refuse consent, and, if granting it, on what conditions. A charge is made for making a planning application.

(a) Development requiring planning permission

The Town and Country Planning Act 1947 took away the right of landowners and occupiers to carry out developments. The nationalisation of this right remains to this day, so that permission is needed for all development unless it is expressly exempted by statute law, as explained below.

"Development": The meaning of "development", though defined (now in TCPA 1990, s 55), has given rise to an abundance of case law and judicial interpretation. Two kinds of activity are covered. Development is—

(i)   carrying out any building, engineering, mining or other operation in, on, over or under land; and

(ii)   making any "material change of use" of any building or land.

Building etc operations: The courts have not considered operations to be developments needing planning permission if they make no physical change to the land, or are temporary or trivial—see *Parkes* v *Secretary of State for the Environment* [1979] 1 All ER 211, where the Court of Appeal held that storing and sorting scrap on land was not an "operation", but it was a "use" of land.

Section 55(1A) of the TCPA 1990 (inserted by s 13 of the Planning and Compensation Act 1991) makes a much needed clarification, stating that "building operations" include "demolition of buildings, rebuilding, structural alterations of or additions to buildings, and other operations normally undertaken by a person carrying on business as a builder". The Secretary of State can direct that the demolition of any specified description of building shall or shall not be development.

Fishing lakes: Planning has become stricter in recent years. In times past the making of fishing lakes, for example, was not treated as development by many a planning officer, but nowadays it will be taken to fall within engineering works, or at least to be a material change of use, as it was decided to be in *Turner* v *Secretary of State for the Environment & Macclesfield BC* [1991] EGCS 104 (CA).

Material change of use: The question whether a change of use is "material" has given difficulty. It is likely to continue to do so. It turns on its effect on "the planning unit" and the courts have said that it is a question of "fact and degree". The identification of the planning unit is not always easy. It is important because, for instance, a use transferred from one part to another part of the same unit will not be a material change of use needing planning consent. In *Burdle* v *Secretary of State for the Environment* [1972] 3 All ER 240, Bridge J said it was a useful working rule to assume that the whole unit of occupation was the planning unit, unless and until some smaller unit could be recognised as the site of activities which amounted in substance to a separate use both physically and functionally.

Another difficulty is that a "change of use" may not be a change of use. In *Brooks and Burton Ltd* v *Secretary of State for the Environment* [1978] 1 All ER 733 (CA), Lawton LJ stated, "We have no doubt that intensification of use can be a material change of use. Whether it is or not depends on the degree of intensification". The court did not decide whether the increased concrete block making in that case was a change of use, because the case was decided on other grounds. Ceasing a use is not a change of use, but the resumption of it again after a period may be (*Hartley* v *Minister of Housing and Local Government* [1970] 1 QB 413).

(b) Exemptions from planning control

The TCPA 1990, s 55(2) lists operations which are to be taken as not involving development. They include, among others, internal works not affecting the external appearance of buildings and the use of buildings on land within the curtilage of a dwellinghouse for any purpose incidental to the enjoyment of the house. No planning permission is therefore needed for these.

Use classes orders: The Secretary of State may make "use classes orders" under section 55(2)(f). Land or buildings used for any purpose within any class specified in the order may be used for any other purpose within the same class without obtaining planning permission. It will not count as development. For example, under the current Use Classes Order 1987 (SI 1987 No 764) Class B7 includes fish curing and rag and bone dealing. It will not be development to start rag and bone dealing on fish-curing premises.

Development orders: An unnecessary burden on the planning authorities and the citizen is avoided by the power given to the Secretary of State to make development orders giving blanket planning permission for types of development specified in the orders. The current General Development Order (much amended by later orders) is SI 1988 No 1813 ("the GDO"). It gives general planning permission for numerous classes of development.

Agriculture and forestry: Perhaps the most significant exemption for our purposes is the use of land, and of buildings occupied with the land, for agriculture or forestry. The farmer does not need planning permission to plough pasture, to grow crops, or to store crops in a barn. He is by no means, however, entirely free from the clutches of the planners. Whilst the GDO (as amended, especially by SI 1991 No 2805) gives planning permission for carrying out on agricultural land building or engineering operations requisite for the agricultural use, limits are placed on the ground area, height and positioning of buildings which may be erected under the blanket permission. For example, the maximum height allowed varies, but at most it is 12 metres, and no part of the building must be within 25 metres of a trunk or classified road. A formula for restricting the ground area of permitted buildings is laid down.

New controls over agriculture and forestry were brought in by amendments to the GDO, and by the Planning and Compensation Act 1991. Most importantly a new Part 6 to Schedule 2 to the GDO, titled "Agricultural Buildings and Operations", was inserted by SI 1991 No 2805. In certain cases (and always in national parks) the farmer must get a ruling from the planning authority as to whether he must get its approval of details of the siting, design and external appearance of buildings before they are constructed.

The Crown: The Crown is not subject to development control. This exemption extends to development carried out by government departments (*Ministry of Agriculture, Fisheries and Food* v *Jenkins* [1963] 2 QB 317—an Agricultural Holdings Act case showing that the change of use of grazing land to afforestation was exempt from planning control not because of the express exemption for afforestation in the Town and Country Planning Acts, but because the Acts did not apply to the Department). There is a non-statutory procedure by which government departments and other bodies with Crown exemption consult planning authorities in advance of developments, and public inquiries are held where a proposal is at variance with the development plan.

Statutory undertakers: Many an Act of Parliament lays down procedures for statutory bodies to obtain official authorisation for works to be carried out in the public interest, or to acquire land or rights under compulsory powers for approved purposes. In such cases it is normal for the authorising Minister to decree deemed planning permission, subject to conditions, when giving consent (see TCPA 1990, s 90). The planning authority is not, however, bypassed in these cases. The planning authority is normally given an opportunity to object, and if it does a public inquiry is held before a decision is made.

Quite complex provisions deal with works carried out on the "operational land" of statutory undertakers. Normally they will be allowed to carry out their statutory purposes, but planning permission is usually applied for under the TCPA 1990. Statutory undertakers as defined in the Act include most bodies giving a public service under statutory powers, like British Rail, British Waterways, British Gas and other licensed gas undertakers, licensed electricity undertakers, and licensed water suppliers, to name but a few.

3. Article 4 Directions

We have seen that blanket planning permission is given by the GDO for specified classes of development. The GDO also enables the local planning authority to turn back the blanket to protect sensitive areas from particular forms of development. Where the planning authority or the Secretary of State is satisfied that development of a particular class should not take place in a particular area without planning consent, it or he may direct that planning permission must be applied for and granted before such development may take place in the area. This is provided by article 4 of the GDO and the directions are known as "Article 4 Directions". A direction by the local planning authority generally needs the Secretary of State's approval.

4. Development plans

The initiative for development does not come from the planning authorities or the Secretary of State, except where they own the land in question, or acquire it compulsorily or by negotiation for development purposes. Control by the planning authorities of development is almost entirely effected by dealing with the initiatives of others when they apply for planning permission. Planning authorities have, however, always attempted positive planning by way of preparing plans. Since 1947 local planning authorities have been required to prepare development plans for their areas and to have regard to them in deciding planning applications.

The original development plans under the Town and Country Planning Act 1947 indicated by maps and statements in great detail "the manner in which a local planning authority propose that land in their area should be used". Areas were allocated for different types of development, or for agriculture or other uses. The phasing of development in development areas was also shown. The procedure for producing the development plans was slow and cumbersome, and from 1968 new-style structure plans giving a broader strategy for counties or other wide areas have been prepared, with local plans of district councils giving the detailed proposals.

Development plans have not ruled with a rod of iron, nor ever could unless the citizen was to be entirely regimented by bureaucracy. There has always been flexibility in planning control, much of it healthy, some of it unpopular. For example, although some areas are earmarked for agriculture, planners must recognise the need to maintain the rural economy and allow diversification where agriculture is in decline, or is discouraged by government. The Planning and Compensation Act 1991 tries to steer planning control towards a more effective plan-led system. The Act requires planning decisions to be made in accordance with current development plans unless there are strong and relevant reasons to depart from them.

In summary, there are the following kinds of development plans.

(a) Structure plans

Broad strategy prepared by county councils in non-metropolitan areas.

(b) Local plans

Made by the non-metropolitan district councils, they translate the broad strategy into detailed planning of districts, identifying areas for different types of land uses, and areas to be kept free from development as open space or green belt or for, say, playing fields.

(c) Unitary development plans

Combined strategic and detailed plans for metropolitan areas, prepared by metropolitan district councils and London boroughs.

National park authorities make national park local plans, and county councils prepare specific waste disposal local plans, and mineral local plans for controlling the winning of minerals, and others as required.

5. Environmental assessments

A technique for the protection of the environment, introduced into the planning system following EC Directive 1986/337, is the environmental assessment ("EA"). The Town and Country Planning (Assessment of Environmental Effects) Regulations 1988 (SI 1988 No 1199) has two schedules of types of development. An EA is mandatory for developments in Schedule 1 in all cases. An EA is needed for developments in Schedule 2 when they are likely to have "significant" environmental effects.

The Secretary of State can require an EA, but primarily the local planning authority decides whether an EA is required should the applicant not volunteer one with his planning application. The applicant can appeal to the Secretary of State against the decision of the local planning authority. Where an EA is required the planning authority must not grant planning permission without taking an EA into account, otherwise the planning permission will be a nullity—though in the dubious decision of Schiemann J in *R v Poole BC ex parte Beebee* [1991] 3 LMELR 60, the judge decided not to quash the planning permission for housing that the local authority gave itself without an EA, as he was satisfied that it had all the relevant environmental information in mind. The EA is not to override all other considerations. The information required to be provided in EAs is laid down in the regulations, together with a procedure and time limits for requiring and producing them.

Only a flavour of the intricate schedules can be given here. Among the developments for which an EA is mandatory are the construction of motorways and other multi-carriageway roads, major railways and airports with runways of not less than 2,100m, nuclear and thermal power stations, large oil refineries and installations for industrial processes involving such things as certain acids and chemicals, asbestos, oil refining and iron and steel smelting (Sch 1). Developments requiring an EA when significant environmental effects are likely include certain agricultural operations involving intensive rearing, new land drainage works, salmon rearing, and lists of other activities under headings such as Chemical

Processes, Energy Industries, Extraction, Food Industries, and Metal Processing (Sch 2).

Whether or not a development falls into one of the two schedules is a decision for the planning authority, not the courts. It can only be challenged by court proceedings on the general principle of administrative law that no reasonable authority could have reached such a decision (in *R* v *Swale BC ex parte Royal Society for the Protection of Birds* [1991] JPL 39, Simon Brown J, applying *Associated Provincial Picture Houses* v *Wednesbury Corporation* [1948] 1 KB 223, decided not to quash a planning consent for land reclamation of 125 acres of a Ramsar site).

6. Planning appeals

An applicant for planning permission has a right of appeal to the Secretary of State if his application is refused, or is granted with conditions unacceptable to him (TCPA 1990, s 78(1)). Appeals are also provided against sundry other planning processes, such as enforcement orders, and in some instances "persons aggrieved" can appeal to the High Court. They can, for example, appeal against development plans and tree preservation orders. There is no right for any person to appeal against the granting of planning permission.

In practice appeals to the Secretary of State are usually determined by an inspector at the Department of the Environment, the Secretary of State only dealing with instances involving policies of particular importance. The appellant or the local planning authority can elect to have a hearing before the appeal is determined. This may be at a local inquiry, but in the vast majority of cases it is done by making written representations.

Except in the special instances where the Act expressly provides for an appeal to the High Court, a planning decision can only be challenged by court proceedings on a point of law. The grant or refusal of planning permission and the other functions of planning authorities are administrative actions outside the jurisdiction of the judiciary. The courts cannot therefore consider the planning merits of a decision, but they can make a declaration that a planning decision or function was wrong in law (*Pyx Granite Co* v *Ministry of Housing and Local Government* [1958] 1 QB 554). A planning decision will be bad in law if the proper procedure was not followed, for example a party to an appeal not being given the opportunity to be heard. Judicial review can, however, be sought where a public authority abuses or exceeds its powers.

7. Enforcement of planning laws

It is not an offence to contravene planning control, but offences are created by the enforcement laws. The TCPA 1990 provides for enforcement in Part VII. It has been strengthened by the Planning and Compensation Act 1991, ss 1 to 11, substituting new versions of several sections and adding some new sections.

(a) Enforcement notices

As of old, planning authorities can serve an enforcement notice on the landowner, occupier or others with a relevant interest, where development needing planning permission is carried out without it, or where there is failure to comply with a condition in a planning consent (TCPA 1990, s 172). Section 173 specifies what must be contained in the notice. There are time limits and fairly straightforward procedures.

Failure to comply with an enforcement notice is an offence carrying a fine up to £20,000 on summary conviction, and unlimited on indictment (s 179). Appeals against enforcement notices may be made to the Secretary of State (s 174) and may result in the notice being upheld, varied or quashed, or planning permission being granted for some or all of the development.

(b) Planning contravention notice

Since January 1992, planning authorities have had a new option which can be pursued without prejudice to the right to serve an enforcement notice. A planning contravention notice may be served if a breach of planning control is suspected. The notice requires information to be given relevant to the planning legality of operations or of land uses. It enables the planning authority to check whether an enforcement notice would be justified, and it gives the owner, occupier or operator an opportunity to offer to apply for planning permission, or to cease an unpermitted activity or otherwise put matters right if they are wrong (s 171C). It is an offence to fail to comply with the notice or to give a false reply (s 171D).

(c) Breach of condition notice

Another new option is to serve a breach of condition notice, where there is a breach of a condition in a planning consent. Failure to comply within the time specified (minimum 28 days) is an offence (s 187A). There is no appeal against the notice.

(d) Stop notices and injunctions

In the past, planning authorities have often been unable to act quickly enough to stop irremediable harm being done in defiance of planning control. Authorities may apply for court injunctions, with the sanction of condign punishment for contempt of court, but an injunction is a discretionary remedy not readily given by the courts. Planning authorities now have a choice of applying either to the county court or the High Court for an injunction to restrain actual or threatened breaches of planning requirements (TCPA 1990, s 187B).

The TCPA 1990 contains a quick remedy in s 183 (as amended by the Planning and Compensation Act 1991). It allows a planning authority to serve a stop notice, either together with an enforcement notice, or

67

afterwards, if it considers that an unpermitted activity specified in the enforcement notice should be halted before the date for compliance with the enforcement notice. The stop notice may prohibit the activity not sooner than three days and not later than twenty-eight days after service. If there are special reasons to justify stopping the activity even earlier, the notice may operate sooner provided that the special reasons are stated. Contravention is an offence carrying a fine up to £20,000 for summary conviction, and an unlimited fine on indictment. A stop notice may not prohibit use of a building as a dwellinghouse, nor prohibit an activity that has continued for four years.

8. Objectors to development

There is no statutory right even for neighbours to object to a planning application except in a few special cases involving "bad neighbour" developments, and certain applications concerning conservation areas and listed buildings (see Chapter 8).

Planning applications are, however, entered on a register open for public examination at the planning authority's offices, and there is no reason why an objector to an application should not make representations to the planning officer or to the chairman or any other member of the planning committee. The existence of an environmental assessment must also be publicised, stating where it may be seen or obtained (SI 1988 No 1199).

(a) "Bad neighbour" developments

Publicity must be given to applications for certain "bad neighbour" developments specified in the GDO. These are activities which may be an exceptional nuisance to neighbours such as the construction of public conveniences, building construction and the operation of knackers yards, sewage treatment works and places of recreation and entertainment. Owners of land affected by such developments are given notice and an opportunity to express objection.

(b) Appeals and public inquiries

An opportunity arises for objection even when the development is not of the likes of knackers yards, when an applicant appeals against the refusal of a planning application, and when for any reason a public inquiry is held. Representations can be made to the inspector. At a public inquiry objectors can put in written evidence, and parties closely affected by the development are entitled also to be heard and to cross-examine witnesses. The inspector uses his discretion to decide whether other objectors should be heard. Busybodies from outside the area cannot expect a platform, but inspectors are anxious not to shut out people with a real interest, and will usually allow local organisations to appear. At the Belvoir Coalfield inquiry, and other major inquiries, the inspector set aside an evening to give any local person who wanted to, a chance to have a say.

Local people can put in formal objections when a local authority proposes to make or to amend a development plan, and anyone may make representations.

B. Protection of agricultural land

It is not the policy in the UK to have a bureaucracy controlling the farming of land. In countries where it has happened under communism it has been a poor advertisement for farming efficiency and protection of the environment. As we have seen, agriculture is to an extent free from planning control. The farmer can choose the type of farming he practises, the crops he grows and to a degree the agricultural operations he carries on. At the same time, as with all industries, there is no shortage of legislation governing what farmers may or may not do in particular respects and localities. Important in this context are management agreements.

1. Management agreements

Management agreements between authorities and owners and occupiers of agricultural land are a means of imposing legally enforceable controls on farming in areas singled out for protection. A management agreement is a flexible friend for all sides, as its terms can be adapted to needs and circumstances. They are not simply negative, prohibiting land uses, but can create positive and useful obligations on the owner and occupier in the public interest, and they provide compensation to the farmer for loss of income occasioned by the restrictions. The agreement can be made "with any person having an interest in the land" (Wildlife and Countryside Act 1981, s 39), but to be effective it needs to be made with the person controlling the land use, and therefore with the landowner or occupier, preferably both.

(a) A general power to make management agreements

This is given to planning and national park authorities and the Broads Authority by section 39 of the Wildlife and Countryside Act 1981 (as amended) "for the purpose of conserving or enhancing the natural beauty or amenity of any land which is both in the countryside and within their area or promoting its enjoyment by the public". It will be "binding on persons deriving title under or from" the person making the agreement (s 39(3)).

(b) On refusal of capital grant

The 1981 Act requires management agreements to be offered to farmers where farm capital grants have been refused due to objections on conservation grounds by a nature conservancy or national park authority (1981 Act, ss 32 and 41). It applies to grant applications in areas notified as sights of special scientific interest, in national parks and in specially notified areas. The management agreement must be offered within three months of the relevant authority receiving the Minister's decision to refuse the grant, and it must contain restrictions on activities endangering the flora, fauna or other features to be protected. It must also provide for payment to the applicant.

(c) Other management agreements

Management agreements can be made also for the benefit of sundry kinds of designated areas and to protect ancient monuments. To summarise:

Sites of special scientific interest—under the 1981 Act, ss 28 and 29, and Countryside Act 1968, s 15 (see Chapter 3, p 31 *et seq.*);

Environmentally sensitive areas—under Agriculture Act 1986, s 18 (Chapter 3, p 38 *et seq.*);

National nature reserves—under National Parks and Access to the Countryside Act 1949, s 16 (Chapter 3, p 36);

Nitrate sensitive areas—under Water Resources Act 1991, s 94 (Chapter 6, p 88).

Ancient monuments—under Ancient Monuments and Archaeological Areas Act 1979, s 17 (Chapters 8 and 9, pp 140 and 157).

(d) Back-up powers

Where management agreements cannot be obtained, the relevant authority can sometimes resort to compulsory purchase of the site (but not in environmentally sensitive areas or nitrate sensitive areas). Compulsory purchase has drawbacks, mainly financial and managerial, ruling it out save in exceptional cases. Management agreements under the 1981 Act can be enforced in civil proceedings and monies paid can be reclaimed if the agreement is not complied with. The orders designating environmentally sensitive areas always require management agreements to contain a right for the Minister, on breach of the agreement, to determine the agreement and recover payments made under it as a civil debt. The same applies to nitrate sensitive areas (SI 1990 No 1013, reg 8).

(e) Payments under management agreements

By s 50 of the 1981 Act the payments to be made by the relevant authority under a management agreement "shall be of such amount as may be determined by the offeror in accordance with guidance given by the Ministers". Guidance has been given in DoE Circulars 4/83 and 6/83.

Payments to tenant farmers should be annual payments reflecting the net profit forgone because of the agreement. Payments to landowners may be lump sums equal to the difference between the restricted and the unrestricted value of the land, or annual payments for loss of profit. The party receiving the offer is entitled, within one month of receiving it, to refer the amount to be determined by arbitration (1981 Act, s 50(3)).

2. Conservation by farm tenants

Approximately one-third of the agricultural land in England and Wales is farmed by tenants. They have obligations to farm efficiently. If they are in breach of their tenancy agreements, or fail to farm in accordance with the Rules of Good Husbandry in section 11 of the Agriculture Act 1947, their security of tenure is imperilled. Practices which may be good for conservation may contravene the Rules of Good Husbandry or the tenancy agreement. In such cases, it is important for the tenant to keep in with his landlord. Management agreements and conservation schemes can therefore be a trap for the unwary tenant. Some procedures give the tenant some protection against falling into the trap, but they are inconsistent in this respect. However, the conservation defences to notices to quit, noted below, encourage conservation and give some protection to tenants.

(a) Environmentally sensitive areas

In the case of management agreements in environmentally sensitive areas, the tenant is required to certify that he has notified the landowner of his intention to make the agreement (Agriculture Act 1986, s 18(6)). This at least points the tenant in the right direction. Unless a management agreement is also made with the landlord, the tenant's management agreement, though enforceable against persons deriving title under or from him (s 18(7)), will not be sufficient when the tenancy ends because the landlord will not derive title from the tenant.

(b) Nitrate sensitive areas

The Water Resources Act 1991, s 95 requires a tenant to obtain the written consent of his landlord before entering into an agreement with the Minister. The tenant will not then be in breach of tenancy in doing anything in compliance with the management agreement (Water Act 1989, Sch 25 para 75 amending the Agricultural Holdings Act 1986). Again, persons deriving title from or under the tenant will be bound by the agreement (s 95(3)), but not the landlord unless he is also coupled in an agreement.

(c) Conservation defence to notice to quit

Tenants of agricultural holdings have security of tenure, virtually for life, under the Agricultural Holdings Act 1986, but "incontestable" notices to quit can be served on them for grounds set out in cases in Schedule 3 to the Act. In three of the cases (Cases C, D and E) which are to do with breaches of tenancy by the tenant, it is stated that anything done in furtherance of a provision in the contract of tenancy for the conservation or enhancement of the natural beauty or amenity of the countryside or the promotion of its enjoyment by the public shall not imperil the tenant's security of tenure. It must be disregarded by a tribunal asked by the landlord to issue a certificate of bad husbandry (Case C), and it will not count as inconsistent with the Rules of Good Husbandry for the grounds of remediable breach of tenancy (Case D) or irremediable breach (Case E).

The Water Act 1989, Sch 25 para 75 added similar protection for the tenant against notices to quit on these three grounds (Cases C, D and E) for anything done in compliance with obligations accepted or imposed by a management agreement in a nitrate sensitive area.

C. Forests, trees and hedgerows

1. Forests

The public manifestly and rightly hold trees to be a national asset to be fostered and increased. So does the Establishment, and not only on amenity grounds. The Forestry Commission rightly states in its brochure, *The Forest Environment* (1991):

> "Much of Britain's wildlife has evolved in forest and woodland habitats. The remaining areas of ancient woodland represent some of the most diverse and valuable ecosystems in Britain, whilst the expanding areas of new forests contain a wide range of both common and rare species".

The trees serve another important purpose, that of absorbing and storing carbon dioxide from the atmosphere.

(a) Community forests

In an imaginative initiative of the Countryside Commission and the Forestry Commission, it is proposed to create 12 community forests on the outskirts of cities and towns, bringing derelict areas back to life and benefiting people, local economies and the national interest. No special legislation is needed. The Countryside Commission has stated that landowners and farmers will be important partners in the development of the forests but there will be no compulsory purchases of land. The Woodland Grant Scheme and the Farm Woodlands Scheme, together with the availability of grants and guidance, are already in place (see Chapter 9).

The aim is for each community forest to be an area for thriving forestry and agriculture, and a place for public education and recreation. The trees will be broadleaved, in the main.

(b) National Forest

The same can be said for the proposed National Forest in the Midlands. Preparations are well under way to create, over 30 years, a forest covering 150 sq miles, in a reincarnation of the ancient forests of Needwood and Charnwood. Thirty million new trees are to be planted and, like the 12 community forests, the accomplishment of the plan will largely depend on local communities and the owners and occupiers of the land.

(c) Storm damage

The work of the Commissions in restoring storm-damaged landscapes, by tree surgery and planting by the Task Force Trees scheme, continues. At least half a million trees have already been planted to repair the damage caused by the great storms in the late 80s and early 90s.

2. Trees

The activities of the Forestry Commission and its unique place in protecting the sylvan environment are referred to in Chapter 2. Grants to encourage private forestry are referred to in Chapter 9. We have seen above that forestry does not come under the control of development by planning authorities. The law, however, has two tools for the protection of trees and woodlands, namely felling control by the Forestry Commission and tree preservation orders.

(a) Felling control

A licence is required from the Forestry Commission to fell trees, other than fruit trees, or trees in a garden, orchard, churchyard or public open space, provided that they are more than 8 cm in diameter (Forestry Act 1967, s 9). No licence is required for felling dead or dangerous trees, trees infected with Dutch elm disease, or trees felled to abate a nuisance. Contravention is an offence under section 17 of the 1967 Act, and the burden of proving that a felling licence is not needed falls on the accused, who must show on a balance of probabilities that one of the exceptions applies (*Forestry Commission* v *Grace* [1992] EG 115, Crown Court).

(b) Tree preservation orders

Tree preservation orders ("TPOs") are made by planning authorities and can be placed on single trees, groups of them and on areas of woodlands, to preserve them in the interests of amenity. The power is exercised under TCPA 1990, ss 198–202, as substantially amended by Planning and Compensation Act 1991, s 23. It is farther-reaching than felling control by the Forestry Commission. A TPO may prohibit cutting down, topping, lopping, uprooting, wilful damage or wilful destruction of trees, except with the consent of the local authority (s 198). A tree unlawfully removed must be replaced with a suitable tree (s 206).

The prohibitions do not apply to dead, dying or dangerous trees, or to growths not meriting the name "tree", such as bushes, scrub, hedgerows and small saplings, though it is not clear when a sapling becomes a tree—compare *Kent County Council* v *Batchelor* (1976) 33 P & CR 185 (CA) with *Bullock* v *Secretary of State for the Environment* (1980) 40 P & CR 246, where Phillips J disagreed with Denning LJ that a woodland tree ought to be over seven or eight inches in diameter to be "a tree". Nor do the prohibitions apply if it is necessary to act to prevent or abate a nuisance, or to comply with a statutory obligation (s 198(6)). On a prosecution, the burden of proving that a tree was dead, dying, dangerous or a nuisance, falls on the accused (*R* v *Alath Construction Ltd & Brightman* (1990) 60 P&CR 533 (CA)).

(c) Appeals

The planning authority can serve a notice requiring replacement by a given date when a tree subject to a TPO is taken down (s 207), and has the right to do so itself and charge the owner if he defaults (s 209), though there is a right of appeal against the notice to the Secretary of State (s 208). There is also a right of appeal against refusal of consent to do any of the forbidden acts. For its part, the planning authority can appeal against felling licences granted by the Forestry Commission for trees subject to TPOs. Appeals are to the Secretary of State.

Guidance emphasising that TPOs are only to be made where removal of trees would have a marked effect on the environment, is given to planning authorities in DoE Circular 36/78. In *Havant BC* v *Taylor* (1992) 7 PAD 329 the Secretary of State allowed an appeal against refusal of consent to fell a mature and healthy tree close to the owner's house in a conservation area, and granted consent subject to the owner planting a smaller species. He considered that the disadvantages to the owner in requiring the tree to remain outweighed the advantage to the public of screening the house from the street.

(d) Procedure

The procedure for making TPOs is in SI 1969 No 17 (amended by SIs 1975 No 148, 1981 No 14, 1988 No 963 and 1990 No 526). An order does not take effect before it is confirmed (s 199). Before confirmation it must be made available for public inspection, copies are to be served on affected owners and occupiers of land and on certain officials. An opportunity is given for objection, and, in the six weeks following confirmation, a TPO may be challenged in the High Court.

(e) Offences

It is an offence to cut down, uproot or wilfully destroy a tree in contravention of a TPO, or to wilfully damage, top, or lop it in a manner likely to destroy it (s 210). Offences carry a maximum fine of £20,000.

Any financial advantage to the defendant in committing the unlawful act must be taken into account in fixing the fine. In *R* v *Razzell* (1990) 12 Cr App R (S) 142 the Court of Appeal upheld fines of £10,000 on each of two counts, and costs of £12,000, for damaging trees subject to TPOs in a conservation area. The defendant's object, partly frustrated by an injunction, was to remove the trees to enable the land to be developed.

(f) Generally

The TCPA 1990 makes provision for compensation to be paid for losses occasioned by refusal of consents (s 203, but see *Bell* v *Canterbury City Council* (1988) 56 P & CR 211 for limits on the scope, and *Deane* v *Bromley BC* [1992] 21 EG 120 for the scope when compensation is justified); for obtaining injunctions to stop threatened offences (s 214A— the county court as well as the High Court has jurisdiction; see *Newport BC* v *Khan* [1990] 1 WLR 1185 (CA)); and for rights of entry to land by authorities (ss 214B, C and D). The equivalent to TPO protection is automatically placed on all trees in a conservation area (see s 211).

A further recourse open to planning authorities is to protect trees by conditions attached to grants of planning permission for development. They are enjoined by TCPA 1990, s 197 to consider it when giving planning permissions.

3. Hedgerows

There is practically no statute law for the preservation of hedges. Hedgerow trees can be protected in the same way as other trees, but not hedgerows as hedgerows. Many a Private Member's Bill has been presented to Parliament in recent years to provide for hedgerow preservation orders, or other means of saving hedgerows from destruction. None has reached the statute book, and when the Government projected some such measures in the Planning and Compensation Bill, they were not pursued.

At the time of writing Mr Peter Ainsworth MP has a Hedgerows Bill before Parliament, but as the Government is believed to be preparing its own Bill for the 1993–94 Session, it is expected that this Private Member's Bill will not be passed. The general scheme of the Bill is that the destruction of a hedgerow on or adjacent to agricultural, forestry or certain other land, shall be an offence, subject to a system of notification to the local authority of an intention to do it. The local authority can then grant consent, or withhold it on statutory grounds, subject to a right of appeal.

(a) Agricultural holdings

Tenants normally covenant in farm tenancy agreements to maintain the hedges on the holding, and the "model clauses" regulations (currently

SI 1973 No 1473) require the tenant "to repair and to keep and leave clean and in good tenantable repair, order and condition" the hedges, along with a list of other "fixed equipment". The "model clauses" are deemed to be incorporated in every tenancy of an agricultural holding except in so far as they are inconsistent with express agreements.

(b) Hedgerow Incentive Scheme

In 1992 the Environment and Countryside Minister, David Maclean, launched the Hedgerow Incentive Scheme to save hedgerows. Ten-year management agreements are offered by the Countryside Commission for the restoration of hedges, the planting of hedges and hedgerow trees and, equally important, for maintenance. Payments will be made towards the cost of the work. The scheme is to be run in close association with the hedgerow grants administered by the Ministry of Agriculture, Fisheries and Food. More details are given in Chapter 9.

D. Mineral workings

Although the law of mines and minerals is too large a subject to deal with in this book, mineral workings have caused such great dereliction to the land surface that the matter is mentioned here to signpost the reader.

"Mining operations in, on, under or over land" are development requiring planning consent, though permitted development rights are given by the GDO to specified ancillary operations. This deemed permission can be overridden in particular instances by Article 4 Directions, or by conditions attached to planning consents. Every county has a Minerals Planning Authority to prepare plans for mineral extractions, usually for a period of ten years, and every county and regional area has a target for production of sand and gravel.

Comprehensive conditions are nowadays always attached to planning consents. The TCPA 1990, s 72(5) and Sch 5 provide for conditions which may be imposed on the grant of planning permission for the winning or working of minerals. The Planning and Compensation Act 1991, s 21 and Sch 1 have substantially amended them and updated the provisions regarding the creation and enlargement of mineral working deposits, aftercare conditions on planning permissions and time limits on permissions for depositing mineral wastes. Mineral working deposits are deposits of material left after minerals have been extracted (see TCPA 1990, s 336(1) as amended). The same section defines minerals as including "all minerals and substances in or under land of a kind ordinarily worked for removal by underground or surface working, except that it does not include peat cut for purposes other than sale".

The registration of old mining permissions deemed to have been granted under Part III of the Town and Country Planning Act 1947 is dealt with by the Planning and Compensation Act 1991, s 22 and Sch 2.

The protection of the land therefore depends to a large extent on restoration conditions attached by the planners to planning permissions. The TCPA 1990, by section 72(5) and Schedule 5, requires an "aftercare condition" to be included where a restoration condition is attached to a planning consent. It will require the land to be restored to agricultural, forestry or amenity use. The applicant has a right of appeal to the Secretary of State against the terms of an aftercare condition (s 78). The Mines and Quarries (Tips) Act 1969 requires tips to be made and kept secure and has sections for preventing danger to the public from disused tips.

(a) Coal

British Coal Corporation mines all but a tiny proportion of the coal extracted in the UK. The Corporation's operations are subject to planning control, as with other mineral extractors, save that the GDO gives British Coal some special permitted development rights. The Government has announced its intention to privatise the coal industry. At the time of writing a Bill is thought to be imminent.

E. Commons

This book is not concerned with public access to land except in so far as it affects conservation. A substantial amount of the countryside is common land, and it has some unique features—one of which is not a right of public access. It is usually not appreciated that common land is simply, as defined in the Commons Registration Act 1965, land subject to rights of common. It is land over which certain local people, the commoners, have rights to be exercised in common. For example, a local person occupying a given property may have the right to graze a given number of sheep on the local common along with similar rights of other inhabitants.

The vast majority of common land in England and Wales is privately owned. There are no public rights to wander at large on it, and the landowners have the ordinary rights of ownership, including the right to evict trespassers. Restrictions on fencing, building and the construction of other works which may impede commoners' rights are placed by the Law of Property Act 1925, s 194 on land which was subject to common rights on 1 January 1926. Such works may only be carried out with the consent of the Secretary of State for the Environment.

There are, however, commons, and village and town greens, that the public have been granted a right to enter for recreation by Acts of Parliament, notably the Metropolitan Commons Act 1866 and local Acts. Such commons are regulated by byelaws.

(a) Management and registration of commons

It has long been the plan to manage commons in an orderly manner. One of the recommendations of the Royal Commission on Common

Land in 1958 was that there should be a scheme of management for every common. In preparation for it the Commons Registration Act 1965 was passed to get all common land and common rights registered. Only land on a commons register is common land, and only registered rights can exist as common rights. Disputed registrations are determined by Commons Commissioners. It was expected that all would be settled within a few years. It did not happen. A large amount of land, not common land at all, was registered by over-enthusiasts, and it is taking decades to sort it all out.

A Common Land Forum, representing most interest groups, made comprehensive recommendations for legislation to achieve proper management of commons, coupled with public access, in the interests of agriculture, protection of the environment and public recreation. Although the Government accepted the report and in 1987 promised legislation, difficulties were found in framing acceptable legislation and no Bill has yet emerged.

F. Treasure trove

From time to time, treasures of great worth and historical interest are discovered in hidden places. In 1992 a hoard of Roman coins, jewellery and silver artefacts was discovered at Hoxne in Suffolk, and in the previous year Bronze Age jewellery was found at Milford Haven, and gold and silver at Snettisham and at Reigate. This has been happening for centuries and the old case of the jewel found in the soot by a chimney sweeper's boy, *Armory* v *Delamirie* (1722) 5 Stra 505, is still the leading case on the rights of a finder. Finds have even included a prehistoric boat embedded in the soil.

(a) The Crown's prerogative

Treasure trove belongs to the Crown under its prerogative, but a find is only treasure trove if it is gold or silver hidden in the earth, or other secret place, and the owner is not known or ascertainable. It was confirmed by the Court of Appeal in *Attorney-General of the Duchy of Lancaster* v *Overton (Farms) Ltd* [1982] 1 All ER 524, concerning third century Roman coins, that treasure trove was limited to the two precious metals and that there must be a substantial amount of gold or silver in the article. As the amount of silver in the coins, was very small, they were not treasure trove.

Further, the find will not be treasure trove unless it was hidden in the past by someone with the intention of recovering it. In *R* v *Hancock* [1990] 3 All ER 183 the accused was convicted of stealing treasure trove in the form of Celtic silver coins that he had found at Warnborough. The Court of Appeal quashed the conviction in the light of expert evidence that the coins were probably votive offerings not intended to be retrieved.

Any person discovering treasure trove must report it to the coroner for the district, who may hold an inquest to determine whether it is treasure trove. The practice is to reward the finder to the full value of the find. Where the discovery is not treasure trove—a Viking boat or a tin of banknotes, for example—and it is found on private land, the presumption is that a landowner with control over the land will have a better claim than a finder (*South Staffordshire Water Co v Sharman* [1869] 2 QB 44—two rings found in a lake).

A Bill is expected in the near future, backed by archaeological and landowning interests, to reform the law of treasure trove and to curb the activities of explorers armed with metal detectors. Although metal detectors have uncovered items which throw light on past history, archaeological sites have also been damaged and plundered.

Chapter 6

Protection of rivers and waters

Abbreviations in this chapter:

NRA	= *National Rivers Authority*
WRA 1991	= *Water Resources Act 1991*
WQO	= *Water quality objective*

NB: For the meaning of "Secretary of State", see page 24.

The privatisation of the water industry in 1989 was undoubtedly a major reform of immense promise for the benefit of our rivers, streams, lakes and bathing waters, to say nothing of human welfare. It did away with the lunatic system whereby major polluters and abstractors had responsibility for pollution and abstraction control, and it created a body with no conflict of interest, the National Rivers Authority ("NRA"), to care for the well-being of our waters. Before privatisation the multi-functional regional water authorities were sewerage and water supply authorities. They were also the pollution and abstraction control authorities, and only they could prosecute for water pollution offences.

The most prevalent polluters were not prosecuted, because the water authorities did not prosecute themselves. They were placed in an impossible position. They inherited an array of overloaded and, in many cases, antique and inefficient sewage treatment works and disposal systems that were polluting rivers and coastal waters, but they were not allowed the resources to put things right. To enable privatisation to take place, the NRA to do its job and the new private companies to be floated, billions of pounds were at long last allocated to rehabilitating sewage treatment works.

About 25 per cent of water supplies was supplied by water companies set up under private Acts. They continued to operate after privatisation.

1. The legislation

Privatisation was effected by the Water Act 1989. Two years later it was repealed and re-enacted, with only minor amendments, along with other watery Acts, in a consolidation of the statute laws into four new Acts. They were the Water Resources Act 1991 ("WRA 1991"), the Water Industry Act 1991, the Statutory Water Companies Act 1991 and the

Land Drainage Act 1991. At the same time the Water Consolidation (Consequential Provisions) Act 1991 was passed to tidy up the transitional and temporary measures, amendments and repeals consequent upon the consolidation. The statute law for England and Wales is now conveniently parcelled up in these 1991 Acts, and in regulations.

In summary, the WRA 1991 deals with the powers and duties of the NRA; the Water Industry Act 1991 with water supply, sewerage and laws relating to the privatised water service companies; the Statutory Water Companies Act 1991 with the water companies created before privatisation by their own individual enabling Acts; and the Land Drainage Act 1991 with the land drainage functions of local authorities and internal drainage boards and with other land drainage laws.

(a) EC legislation

Some laws in the 1991 Acts implement EC directives. In turn the EC is a party to international treaties against marine pollution, including the Treaty of Bonn for Dealing with Pollution of the North Sea by hydrocarbons, and the conventions against marine dumping (Oslo 1972) and marine pollution from land-based sources (Paris 1974). EC directives for protection of waters are manifold. They are well summarised in other works (such as Howarth's *Water Pollution Law* and Hughes' *Environmental Law*). They are mostly anti-pollution measures. Minimum standards are set for different kinds of waters. Some of the most significant for our subject are the Dangerous Substances Directive (1974/464), the Groundwater Directive (1980/68), Surface Water Directive (1975/440), Water Quality Objectives Directive (1978/659), the Drinking Water Directive (1980/778), the Bathing Water Directive (1976/160) and directives stemming from them.

2. Effect of privatisation

The 1989 privatisation separated the regulatory functions of the regional water authorities from their water supply and sewerage duties. The ten water authorities in England and Wales were translated into private limited companies, licensed, regulated and overseen by a Director-General of Water Services and to some degree by the Secretary of State for the Environment. These plcs were given water supply and sewerage duties. The previous statutory water companies continued under regulation by the Director-General. The regulatory functions of the former water authorities were passed to the new NRA bolstered with new duties and a strong brief to care for and improve inland and coastal waters.

(a) Conservation duties

All concerned are required to promote conservation. Section 2(2) of the WRA 1991 places a duty on the NRA to promote the conservation and enhancement of the natural beauty and amenity of inland and coastal waters and land associated with them, and the conservation of flora and fauna dependent on the aquatic environment. Section 16 follows up with an elaborate conservation duty placed on the Secretary of State and the Minister of Agriculture in formulating or considering proposals relating to the NRA. The Water Industry Act 1991, s 3 places a corresponding duty on these Ministers, the Director-General of Water Services and every water service plc. Provisions in the 1991 Acts regarding sights of special scientific interest and Codes of Practice are noted in Chapter 3.

All this is very much to the good. At last, in the WRA 1991 we have a code for the protection and improvement of the aqueous environment, and, in the NRA, an authority willing and bent on achieving it, but already the Government has brought out the melting pot again, announcing its intention to form a new Environment Agency, stating that "the new agency will bring together all of the functions of the NRA, Her Majesty's Inspectorate for Pollution and the waste regulation work of local authorities" (DoE Press Release, 15 July 1992). It remains to be seen whether this will be a boon or a setback.

3. The National Rivers Authority

In a nutshell the NRA's statutory responsibilities are:

(a) protection of water quality (pollution control);
(b) protection of water resources (abstraction control);
(c) flood defence;
(d) fisheries;
(e) some recreation duties;
(f) some navigation duties; and
(g) the conservation duties noted above (WRA 1991, s 2).

It has a general duty to make arrangements for research (s 2(3)).

The NRA is given power to acquire land and rights for its purposes, by agreement or compulsory purchase, to carry out works, including works to prevent or rectify pollution (ss 161 and 162), and to construct pipelines in streets and other land (ss 154–168 and Sch 18 and 19). It is given powers of entry to premises and vessels for certain purposes (ss 169–174 and Sch 20), and powers to make and enforce byelaws for sundry purposes (ss 210 and 211 and Sch 25 and 26). Byelaws, as always, have to be confirmed by a Minister.

(a) Constitution of the NRA

The NRA consists of no fewer than eight or more than fifteen members (including the chairman). Two are appointed by the Minister of Agriculture, Fisheries and Food and the remainder by the Secretary of State for the Environment. It is divided into ten regions. Each region has a general manager. There is no provision in the Act for regional boards, but in practice each region has one. The NRA is required to have regional rivers advisory committees (s 7), regional fisheries advisory committees, and such local fishery advisory committees as it deems necessary (s 8), and regional flood defence committees (s 9). The Secretary of State is required to maintain an advisory committee for Wales (s 6).

4. Water pollution control

(a) Common law

Before examining the statute law, it should be noted that hitherto the most effective weapon against water pollution has been the common law action, or threat of it, for damages and an injunction.

At common law a riparian owner is entitled to have the water running through his land unchanged from its natural state in quality or quantity. It is a nuisance giving a cause of action if a person owning, occupying or having an interest in water is caused loss or damage by another person or body changing its quality. The courts over the ages have been strong in enforcing this law.

The rule in *Rylands* v *Fletcher* (1868) LR 3 HL 330 (reported at first instance as *Fletcher* v *Rylands* (1866) LR 1 Ex 265) is examined in Chapter 4, p 43. Stating the rule, Blackburn J said—

"the person who for his own purposes brings onto his land and collects and keeps there anything likely to do mischief if it escapes, must keep it in at his peril, and, if he does not do so, is *prima facie* answerable for all the damage which is the natural consequence of its escape".

Chief Justice Holt put it more succinctly 163 years earlier in *Tenant* v *Goldwin* (1703) Lord Raym 1089, saying: "He whose filth it is must keep it in".

Consent to discharge a polluting substance under Part III of the WRA 1991 (see below), though a defence to a criminal charge, is not a defence to a civil action for nuisance or negligence.

(b) Multiple pollutions

It is no defence to a civil action for a person discharging effluent into a river to show that others were contributing to the pollution (*Crossley & Sons* v *Lightowler* (1867) 16 LT 4338).

(c) Disclosure of trade secrets

The NRA has recognised the value of civil actions in halting pollutions and getting the miscreants to pay for restoration. It has proved co-operative not only in using its expertise and knowledge to get damaged fisheries restored, but also in advancing claims. It must be noted, however, that the NRA is prohibited by WRA 1991, s 204 from disclosing information that it has gleaned under its statutory powers about the affairs of a business or an individual, unless the business or individual consents.

(d) Pollution offences

Part III of the WRA 1991 sets out a series of pollution offences. The prosecutor is usually the NRA, but there is no longer a legal restriction preventing private prosecutions. The Anglers' Co-operative Association (a remarkably successful anti-pollution body) has, for example, secured convictions against sewage authorities in recent years. From its first day in 1989 the NRA showed its intention to prosecute without fear or favour, by charging Shell with pollution of the Mersey with oil. A fine of £1m was obtained.

It is an offence under section 85 of the WRA 1991 to cause or knowingly permit—

(i) any poisonous, noxious or polluting matter or any solid waste matter to enter any "controlled waters"; or

(ii) any trade or sewage effluent to be discharged into any controlled waters, or from land, through a pipe, into the sea outside the seaward limits of controlled waters; or

(iii) any trade or sewage effluent to be discharged, contrary to a prohibition from the NRA under section 86 (see below), or likewise any prescribed substance, or prescribed concentration of substances, or effluent from a prescribed process, from a building or any fixed plant onto or into land, or into any waters of a lake or pond which are not "inland freshwaters"; or

(iv) any matter to enter any inland freshwaters so as to tend (either directly, or in combination with other matter) to impede the proper flow of the waters in a manner leading, or likely to lead, to a substantial aggravation of pollution due to other causes, or of the consequences of such pollution; or

(v) (by s 90(2)) a substantial amount of vegetation to be cut or uprooted in or near any inland freshwaters and to fail to take reasonable steps to remove any that is in the water.

Section 86, referred to in (iii) above, allows the NRA, by notice, to prohibit, or place conditions on discharges. No notice shall apply to discharges from a vessel (s 86(3)). Section 87 sets out some special rules regarding criminal liability and defences as regards the offences in (ii) and (iii) above, relating to discharges into and from sewers.

It is an offence under section 90(1) to cause, without the NRA's consent, a deposit in an inland freshwater, accumulated by reason of a dam, weir or sluice, to be carried away in suspension in the water.

(e) Definitions

Some of the terms of art used are defined in section 104 of WRA 1991, which Parliamentary draftsmen have managed to make extraordinarily complex. Practitioners will need to examine the section for precise meanings. The following explanations may suffice otherwise.

(f) "Controlled waters"

These include territorial waters up to three nautical miles from coastal baselines; coastal waters, including rivers below the freshwater limit and including enclosed docks; "inland freshwaters", being rivers and watercourses above the freshwater limit, and lakes or ponds which discharge into a river or watercourse or into another lake or pond which so discharges; and any waters contained in underground strata.

A "lake or pond" includes a reservoir (s 104(3)). A lake or pond which does not discharge as described above, and any area of the territorial sea, may count as controlled waters if the Secretary of State so decrees by order. Equally he can decree that lakes or ponds or watercourses of a description given in an order shall not count as controlled waters (s 104(4)).

(g) "Causes or knowingly permits"

This phrase has been interpreted by the courts in a number of cases. The offence of causing the entry of a pollutant can be committed even if there is no intention to do so, and no negligence. When leaves blocked the intake of a pump, through nobody's negligence, so that effluent overflowed from a tank into a river, the House of Lords held that the offence had been committed (*Alphacell* v *Woodward* [1972] 2 All ER 475).

A person does not, however, "cause" pollution when it is due to the act of another unauthorised person, as where a trespasser opened the valve of a fuel storage tank (*Impress (Worcester) Ltd* v *Rees* [1971] 2 All ER 357), but a person "knowingly permits" a pollution if he could stop another causing it, but does nothing (cf *Lockhart* v *NCB* (1981) SCCR 9). The Court of Appeal in *Wychavon DC* v *National Rivers Authority* [1993] 1 WLR 125 decided that the local authority did not "cause" pollution by failing to discover promptly the source of a discharge of sewage into a river, or by failing to clear a blockage as soon as possible when it was discovered. It might have "knowingly permitted" the pollution, but it was not charged with that.

(h) Penalties

On conviction of an offence under section 85 the offender is liable on summary conviction to receive imprisonment up to three months, or a fine not exceeding £20,000 or both; and on conviction on indictment to imprisonment up to two years, or an unlimited fine, or both.

(i) Defences

Sections 88 and 89 set out a number of defences to the pollution offences. It is a defence to a charge under section 85 if the entry or discharge of any matter is in accordance with a discharge consent given by the NRA, or by the Secretary of State in lieu, as referred to below (s 88(1)(a)). It is not an offence if the entry or discharge is made in an emergency to avoid danger to life or health, provided that all reasonably practicable steps are taken to minimise the polluting effect and particulars are given to the NRA as soon as practicable (s 89(1)).

The sections also exonerate those who discharge under certain statutory provisions, authorisations and licences. Discharge of trade or sewage effluent from a vessel (s 89(2)) and water from an abandoned mine (s 89(3)) is not an offence.

(j) Discharge consents

Pollution control depends to a large extent on the system of consenting to discharges into waters. In the past consents have too often been licences to pollute. Schedule 10 to the WRA 1991 sets out the procedures. Applications for consents must be made to the NRA. The NRA must publicise all applications in local papers and the *London Gazette* and send copies to each local authority and water undertaker for the area concerned, unless the Secretary of State certifies that the public interest or trade secrets would be unreasonably prejudiced thereby. Objections may be made, and if the NRA is minded to give consent, it must notify anyone who has objected. Any objector may then invite the Secretary of State to call in the application for his own decision, which he may do under para 4 of Schedule 10. If he does, he may, in his discretion, hold a public inquiry or a hearing.

Consent may be given, whether by the NRA or the Secretary of State, unconditionally or subject to conditions, or it may be refused. The NRA has a duty to review consents from time to time, and it has power to revoke, modify or impose conditions. Appeals against refusal of consent, revocation or modification or against conditions attached to consents, may be made to the Secretary of State under section 91. Annual charges are now made for discharge consents by the NRA under section 131.

The Salmon and Freshwater Fisheries Act 1975, s 4, contains an offence of polluting waters containing fish, but qualifications in the section have caused difficulties and it is seldom used.

(k) Water quality objectives

Part of the strategy of the WRA 1991 for the improvement and maintenance of water quality, and for compliance with EC directives, is to set water quality objectives ("WQOs"). WQOs will be set for all "controlled waters" in due course, starting with rivers, because a classification system already exists for them.

The Secretary of State starts by prescribing in regulations a system of classifying waters by reference to the purposes for which they are to be suitable, to substances that are to be present, or absent, and other characteristics (s 82). At the time of writing (November 1993) the Government have issued a consultation paper with draft regulations, planned to come into force in 1994, proposing a new system of classifying river quality in England and Wales for the purposes of setting WQOs. There would be six classes of river quality (FE1 to FE6) assessed from samples taken in accordance with prescribed procedures. The classification for any water will depend on the dissolved oxygen content, biochemical oxygen demand, total ammonia, un-ionised ammonia, pH value, dissolved copper and total zinc. The regulations are to be titled The Surface Waters (Fisheries Ecosystem) (Classification) Regulations 1993 (SI number not yet allocated).

The Secretary of State establishes WQOs by notifying them to the NRA. He may review WQOs at intervals of not less than five years after notification, or at any time if requested by the NRA (s 83). A duty is placed on the Secretary of State and the NRA to achieve and maintain WQOs by way of exercising their pollution control powers, and the NRA has a duty to monitor the extent of pollution in "controlled waters" (s 84). In reality, the NRA does the donkey work of research and planning and much of the consultation. The object is to complete the task of setting WQOs in or before 1995, with targets of three to five years for achieving them.

(l) Public registers

A valuable adjunct to the pollution laws, especially for voluntary bodies performing a watchdog role, are the public registers established, though tardily, under the Control of Pollution Act 1974 and now under WRA 1991, s 190. The NRA is required to enter on the registers all notices of water quality objectives, applications for discharge consents, discharge consents given, including conditions attached to them, and full information regarding samples taken under the Act of effluents or waters and various other information.

The registers must be made available for public examination free of charge at all reasonable times, and facilities for taking copies of entries at a reasonable fee must be afforded (s 190(2)).

(m) Water protection zones

The Secretary of State is given power by section 93 of the WRA 1991 to designate water protection zones where he is satisfied it is appropriate, with a view to preventing or controlling the entry of any poisonous, noxious or polluting matter into "controlled waters", and thereby to prohibit or restrict the carrying on of activities likely to result in the pollution of the waters. Designation is by order specifying the zone and the activities which are prohibited or restricted. The order may make it an offence to contravene the order. It may empower the NRA to decide the activities that the order shall apply to, and may leave it to the NRA to give or withhold consent to prescribed activities. Designations are not to be used to control the leaching of nitrate from agricultural land. This is tackled separately.

(n) Nitrate sensitive areas

The Minister of Agriculture, Fisheries and Food and the Secretary of State for Wales may designate areas of land as nitrate sensitive areas ("NSAs") with the object of preventing or controlling the leaching of nitrate from agricultural land into "controlled waters" (for meaning see above, p 85). By WRA 1991 s 94, the designating order, or a subsequent order, may specify activities which must be carried out in the area, or activities which are prohibited or restricted. For example, the application of fertilisers may be banned, or even arable farming. An order can make contravention a criminal offence (s 94(4)(d)).

The aim is for the Minister or the Secretary of State for Wales to enter into agreements with landowners and farmers to farm in a specified manner in return for annual payments to compensate for the loss of income involved. A tenant requires the consent of the landowner to enter into an agreement (s 95(2)(b)). An agreement under these provisions is binding on all successors in title of the person making the agreement (s 95(3)).

The farming bodies have accepted the NSA system as a fair way of tackling the problem of nitrate leaching, but they question the aptness of the widespread restrictions envisaged by the EC Nitrate Directive of 1991, under which "vulnerable zones" are to be identified on the basis of criteria believed, on the scientific evidence, to be unnecessarily stringent.

(o) Code of good agricultural practice

The Ministry of Agriculture, Fisheries and Food produced in 1991 a Code of Good Agricultural Practice for the prevention of farm pollutions. It specifies good practices for the storage and use of agricultural waste, slurry, manure, silage, fertiliser, fuel oil, pesticides and other possible pollutants, and sundry practices for avoiding pollution. It is now a statutory code under WRA 1991, s 97. Contravention does not give rise to civil or criminal liability, but may be taken into account by the NRA in the exercise of its powers.

Farmers are entitled to one free advisory visit on the prevention of pollution from the Agricultural Development and Advisory Service.

5. Protection of water resources—abstraction and impounding control

In the decades preceding water privatisation the authorities presided over a nationwide lowering of flows in rivers. Many a river, like the Darent, the Ver and the Piddle, once proud in depth, has been reduced to a dried bed, or at best a trickle in wet seasons. Mostly it was not due to natural causes, but by massive abstraction of water to quench the thirst of domestic households, commerce and industry. Possibly the most formidable task confronting the NRA is to devise and implement methods and policies to reverse the decline and to replenish and protect water resources which have been allowed to decline.

(a) Common law rights

A riparian owner is entitled at common law to take and use water flowing through or past his land, or in underground channels. The right is to take all he needs for ordinary domestic purposes and for livestock, but otherwise he must not diminish the quantity of water flowing to other properties. The common law right is curtailed by the controls on abstraction in the WRA 1991, Part II.

(b) NRA's duty

A duty of general management of water resources is placed on the NRA, whereby it is to take all actions necessary or expedient for the purposes of conserving, redistributing, augmenting, and securing the proper use of, water resources in England and Wales. In so doing it must comply with any directions given by the Secretary of State (s 19). It has a duty "so far as reasonably practicable" to enter into schemes with water undertakers to secure the proper management and operation of water sources, including reservoirs (s 20), and it is responsible for licensing abstraction and impoundment.

(c) Minimum acceptable flows and levels

The system for fixing minimum acceptable flows for rivers, as a yardstick for determining what abstractions should be permitted, has existed since 1963, but there has been a total dereliction of duty in this respect. It is rumoured that a minimum acceptable flow was once set somewhere. If so, it was the only one. The challenge is now handed to the NRA by section 21 of the WRA 1991, but in a sense it is too late and too soon to tackle it, because flows have deteriorated so much that there is no point in setting minimum acceptable flows until a means of achieving them can be worked out.

The scheme of the Act is that the NRA "may, if it thinks it appropriate to do so" submit a draft statement to the Secretary of State with regard to any inland water, other than a "discrete water" (namely, land-locked; see s 221) with a formula for fixing the minimum acceptable flow. Section 21 sets out a range of factors to be taken into account, and bodies to be consulted. Schedule 5 lays down a procedure for notifying all

89

and sundry, and for giving or withholding approval by the Secretary of State.

The Act states that the minimum flow specified shall not be less than the minimum which, in the opinion of the NRA, is needed for safeguarding the public health, and for meeting the requirements of existing lawful uses for agriculture, industry, water supply or other purposes, and the requirements of navigation, fisheries and land drainage (s 21(5)). The Secretary of State may direct the NRA to consider whether a minimum acceptable flow should be determined for a particular inland water and to reply either with the answer no, or with a draft statement of provisions for determining the flow (s 22).

The same exercise may be gone through to fix a minimum acceptable level or volume of water in an inland water (s 23). Where a minimum acceptable flow or level has been fixed, the NRA in dealing with a licence to abstract shall have regard to the need to secure that the flow at any control point will not be reduced below the minimum fixed, or if it is already below, to secure that it will not be further reduced (s 40).

(d) Abstraction and impounding offences

It is an offence under section 24 of the WRA 1991 to abstract water from any "source of supply", or to cause or permit any other person to do so, except in pursuance of an abstraction licence.

In the case of water in underground strata it is an offence, without a licence, to begin, or to cause or permit any other person to begin, to construct or extend a well, borehole or other work for abstracting the water, or to take measures to abstract additional quantities of water from the strata.

Likewise it is an offence for any person to begin, or cause any other person to begin, to construct or alter any impounding works at any point in an inland water, unless the water is land-locked, or an impounding licence is held, or the works will not obstruct or impede the flow of the water (s 25).

It is also an offence to contravene any condition or requirement of an abstraction or impounding licence.

None of these offences is committed in the cases where no abstraction or impounding licence is needed (see below).

The penalty on summary conviction of any of the offences is a fine not exceeding the statutory maximum (currently £5,000—Criminal Justice Act 1991, s 17). On indictment it is an unlimited fine.

(e) "Source of supply"

To arrive at the meaning of "source of supply" it is necessary to consider its definition, and the definitions of some of its ingredients, "inland water", "discrete water" and "underground strata", in section 221(1) and (3). When they are jig-sawed together it means a river, stream or watercourse; a lake, pond (natural or artificial), reservoir or dock; a channel, creek, bay, estuary or arm of the sea; and water in any underground strata, well, borehole or similar work, or adit or passage connected therewith—except that a lake, pond or reservoir not discharging into another inland water is not a source of supply, and therefore no licence is needed to abstract from it. In the case of a group of two or more lakes, ponds or reservoirs and any watercourses connecting them, none is a "source of supply" so long as none discharges to any inland water outside the group.

(f) "Abstraction"

Section 221(1) states that:

"'abstraction', in relation to water contained in any source of supply, means the doing of anything whereby any of that water is removed from that source of supply, whether temporarily or permanently, including anything whereby the water is so removed for the purpose of being transferred to another source of supply".

The Court of Appeal in *British Waterways Board* v *National Rivers Authority*, The Times, 4 August 1992 held that it was not an abstraction from a canal, requiring a licence, when a farmer abstracted water, under an abstraction licence, from an outfall channel (not part of the canal) causing water from the canal to flow by gravity into the outfall channel.

(g) When no licence is needed

No licence is needed for abstractions of small amounts of water as follows—

(i) an abstraction not exceeding 5 cu m (approx 1,100 galls) if it is not part of a continuous operation, or a series of operations—but the NRA can consent to an increase of this exemption up to 20 cu m in any case (s 27(1) and (2));

(ii) an abstraction not exceeding 20 cu m (approx 4,400 galls) in any 24-hour period, of water other than groundwater, for use on a contiguous holding for agricultural purposes, but not spray irrigation; or of underground or surface water for the domestic purposes of the occupier's own household on contiguous land (s 27(3), (4) and (5)).

The Act gives rights to abstract water without a licence in the course of, or resulting from, land drainage operations; or to prevent interference with mining, quarrying, engineering, building or other such operations; or to prevent damage to works from any such operations (s 29); and there are exemptions for navigation, harbour and conservancy authorities (s 26); for fire fighting (s 32(2)); and for vessels (s 32(1)). Some special rules where the exemptions apply to wells, boreholes and the like can be found in sections 27(7), 28, 29(4), 30 and 32(3).

(h) Abstraction and impounding licences

The WRA 1991 contains lengthy provisions regarding licences in sections 34 to 63, but it is not necessary to mention them in any detail here. Applications for licences are to be in a prescribed form and in accordance with regulations. Notice must be given to the national park planning authority if a national park is affected (s 34). Publicity must be given in the *London Gazette* and local newspapers, and the public must be given the opportunity to inspect the application free of charge and to make representations (s 37), and copies of applications must be served on certain authorities and undertakers.

In considering applications the NRA must take into account representations made to it, for example by objectors, and also existing rights of others (s 38), river flows and any minimum acceptable flows (s 40). The Secretary of State may call in applications for his own decision (ss 41 and 42) and there is provision for appeals to the Secretary of State from decisions of the NRA (ss 43 and 44).

An abstraction licence gives a right to abstract to the extent authorised by it, and it is a defence to a civil action against a licence holder in respect of the abstraction that it was done in accordance with a licence, though not actions for negligence or breach of contract (s 48). Provision is made for licences to be passed on in the event of a change of occupation (ss 49 and 50), and for revocation and modification of licences (ss 51–62) and for certain licences of right (s 65 and Sch 7). The owner of fishing rights may apply for a licence to be varied or revoked once it has been running for at least one year, provided that no minimum acceptable flow has been fixed for the water concerned (s 55).

The NRA can and does make a charge for licences, and for applications for licences, but not for licences to abstract underground water for agricultural purposes, other than spray irrigation, where the abstractions are not to exceed 20 cu m per 24 hours.

(i) Drought orders

A useful shot in the locker for protecting water supplies is the power to make drought orders under sections 73–81 of the WRA 1991. Although they are made by the Secretary of State, he can only make an order on the application of the NRA or a water undertaker (s 73(3)).

When there is an exceptional shortage of rain, or a serious deficiency of water supplies exists or is threatened in an area, the Secretary of State may make "an ordinary drought order" for the area. Orders may, among other things, prohibit or limit the taking of water from specified sources, or the use of water for specified purposes (for example, hose pipe bans), and may authorise the NRA or a water undertaker to take water from specified sources, or to discharge water to specified places (s 74). An ordinary drought order can be made for a maximum of six months in the first place, but it may be extended up to one year from the date it came into force (s 74(3) and (4)). A drought order may authorise the NRA or a water undertaker to do works specified in the order and to enter any land to do so after giving a minimum of 24 hours' notice to the occupier (s 78).

In the event of an exceptional drought "likely to impair the economic or social well-being of persons" in an area, the Secretary of State can make a more stringent "emergency drought order" (s 73(2)), prohibiting or limiting the use of water and authorising water supply by standpipes or water tanks, and to set them up in streets (s 75). Emergency orders can be made for a maximum of three months, but they can be extended to a total of five months.

It is an offence to contravene a drought order, but it is a defence for the accused "to show that he took all reasonable precautions and exercised all due diligence to avoid the commission of the offence". The penalty on summary conviction is a fine not exceeding the statutory maximum (currently £5,000—Criminal Justice Act 1991, s 17), and on indictment an unlimited fine (s 80).

6. Flood defence

The NRA is given by Part IV of the WRA 1991 a duty of "general supervision over all matters relating to flood defence" (s 105) and it must arrange for all its flood defence functions to be carried out by regional flood defence committees (s 106).

(a) "Flood defence"

This means the drainage of land and the provision of flood warning systems, and "drainage" includes defence against water, including sea water, irrigation (other than spray irrigation) and warping (s 113(1)).

(b) Land drainage functions

The internal drainage boards continue to carry out land drainage functions as regards watercourses which do not rank as "main river". The NRA exercises, through executive committees, the powers given in the Land Drainage Act 1991 in relation to main rivers. A "main river" is simply a watercourse shown as a main river on a main river map (s 113(1)).

(c) Structures and main rivers

By section 109, no person is allowed to erect any structure in, over or under a main river, or any structure for containing or diverting floodwaters of a main river, except with the consent of the NRA and in accordance with plans and sections approved by the NRA. If any person does so without consent, the NRA may remove, alter or pull it down and recover the cost from the malefactor.

Land drainage byelaws usually require the NRA's consent to be obtained before any work is done to a river or stream or to the banks.

7. Control of fisheries

The well-being of a water as a fishery is nearly always a sound gauge of the quality of the water. The fishery function of the NRA is crucial to its conservation duty. Section 114 of the WRA 1991 states quite simply, "It shall be the duty of the Authority [NRA] to maintain, improve and develop salmon fisheries, trout fisheries, freshwater fisheries and eel fisheries".

The NRA is required to establish and maintain fishery advisory committees, of persons who are not members of the Authority, and to consult them as to the manner in which it is to perform its duty under s 114 (s 8(1)).

The fishery programme of the NRA in 1992 involved expenditure of some £24m, of which £11m was derived from fishing licences and duties, and the balance from the Treasury (Corporate Plan 1992/93). The NRA proposed to levy contributions on fishery owners and occupiers towards the cost of performing its duty to maintain, improve and develop fisheries. This power has existed since 1923 but has scarcely been operated, partly because it involved double rating. A fishery is now exempt from rating when a fishery contribution is levied (Local Government Finance Act 1988, Sch 5). The proposal has, however, been abandoned. Charges for fishing licences are to be increased instead.

The laws for the government of angling are mainly in the Salmon and Freshwater Fisheries Act 1975 (much amended by the Water Act 1989 and other Acts, and some of it translated into the WRA 1991). Its provisions outlaw certain methods of taking or destroying fish, deal with the obstruction of the passage of fish in waters, close seasons, fishing licences, regulation of fisheries, and powers of bailiffs and other officials (see pp 122-123 below).

8. The canals

There are over 2,000 miles of canals in England, Wales and Scotland. They represent a great public amenity, a source of recreation, a means of passage, and also a rich heritage of structures, buildings and artefacts of historical, architectural and engineering interest. The canals in England and Wales are "controlled waters" as defined in the WRA 1991 and therefore within the jurisdiction of the NRA for water quality and abstraction control, but responsibility for the management of the canal system throughout England, Wales and Scotland falls to the British Waterways Board.

British Waterways has its own statutory environmental watchdog, the Inland Waterways Amenity Advisory Council (IWAAC), created by the Transport Act 1968, s 110. A relatively small part of the system, though not unimportant, consists of commercial waterways for carrying freight.

Most of the system is designated by the Transport Act 1968 as "cruising waterways" used mainly for recreation. A function of IWAAC is to advise the Board and the Minister on any proposal to add to or reduce the cruising waterways. In practice its main work is another of its statutory functions, namely:

"to consider, and, where it appears to them to be desirable, to make recommendations to the Waterways Board *or* the Minister with respect to any matter—
(i)   affecting the use or development for amenity or recreational purposes, including fishing, of the cruising waterways;
(ii)   with respect to the provisions for those purposes of services or facilities in connection with those [the cruising] waterways or the commercial waterways" (s 110(2)).

Chapter 7

Protection of wildlife

Abbreviations in this chapter:

1975 Act	= *Salmon and Freshwater Fisheries Act 1975*
1981 Act	= *Wildlife and Countryside Act 1981*
MAFF	= *Ministry of Agriculture, Fisheries and Food*
NRA	= *National Rivers Authority*

NB: For the meaning of "Secretary of State", see page 24.

1. The approach to species protection

The laws for species protection are complex. An outline of the strategy of the laws is therefore given here, before considering them in more detail.

The general approach of the law for the protection of birds, animals and plants is to visit criminal liability on malefactors who interfere unduly with wildlife and habitats. Protection is also achieved by some of the designations described in Chapter 3, especially in sites of special scientific interest, nature reserves, "Ramsar sites" (wetlands of international importance) and special protection areas under the EC Birds Directive 79/409, though the protection is limited.

There are always exceptions, but by and large an offence is committed when harm is done to wildlife, or at least to species that the law considers it necessary to conserve. These penal laws are against killing, taking or destroying species of animals or birds, or disturbing them when they are most vulnerable, that is in their breeding seasons or when young are being reared. The taking or destruction of certain wild plants is made an offence, as is the introduction into the wild of unwelcome birds, beasts, fishes and plants. These prohibitions are underpinned by laws against possessing, buying and selling, advertising for sale and importing protected species living or dead. Certain methods of killing or taking are also outlawed.

Protection for the rarest creatures and plants is stringent throughout the year, whilst others are protected only during close seasons, when they are breeding or rearing young, but it is never absolute. Exceptions are made for humane killing, for the protection of crops and for other reasons.

The rights of people deriving their livelihood from the land and of the holders of sporting rights are recognised. They are exempt to some degree from criminal liability.

2. The legislation

The protective laws are mainly found in Part I of the Wildlife and Countryside Act 1981 ("the 1981 Act"). Practitioners should check that they are using an updated version, as the 1981 Act has been amended by the Wildlife and Countryside (Amendment) Acts of 1985 (amending s 28) and 1991 (amending ss 5 and 11). The Water Act 1989 amended sections 27(1) and 36(7), and repealed section 48. Schedules 8 and 9 to the Environmental Protection Act 1990 made sundry other amendments: a new section 27A was added, and section 38 and Schedule 13 para 5 were repealed.

An amendment to section 24 requires the lists of protected animals and plants in Schedules 5 and 8 to be reviewed every five years from 30 October 1991.

(a) Variation of 1981 Act schedules

Section 22 of the 1981 Act allows ministerial variation of the lists of birds, animals and plants in the schedules. This has been done by the Wildlife and Countryside Act 1981 (Variation of Schedules) Orders of 1988 (SI 1988 No 288 adding 19 animals to Sch 5 and 31 plants to Sch 8, and increasing the protection of certain animals); of 1989 (SI 1989 No 906 adding 22 butterflies to Sch 5); of 1991 (SI 1991 No 367 amending Sch 5); and of 1992 (SI 1992 Nos 320 and 2674 amending Sch 9, SI 1992 No 2350 adding animals and plants to Sch 5 and 8, and SI 1992 No 3010 removing certain birds from Sch 2 and 3).

(b) Other legislation

Deer, badgers and seals have their own separate legislation. The Game Acts 1828–1960 are anti-poaching measures, more for the benefit of the owners of sporting rights than for species protection as such. They include the Ground Game Act 1880 designed to allow farmers with no shooting right to protect their crops from the ravages of hares and rabbits. Additionally there is legislation prohibiting the import and export of endangered species. Bats are given individual attention in the 1981 Act.

We will consider in detail the measures to safeguard wild birds, animals, plants, fish and endangered species.

A. Wild birds

1. Two basic offences

The 1981 Act is the main instrument for the protection of wild birds in the law of England, Wales and Scotland. It protects all wild birds of whatever species, except so far as the Act itself, or orders made under it, makes or make exceptions. It starts by creating two offences. For convenience of explaining these intricate laws, they will be referred to as "the two basic offences".

(a) Interference with birds, nests and eggs

First, the Act makes it an offence:

"if any person intentionally—

(a) kills, injures or takes any wild bird;

(b) takes, damages or destroys the nest of any wild bird while that nest is in use or being built; or

(c) takes or destroys an egg of any wild bird" (s 1(1)).

(b) Unlawful possession of birds and eggs

Secondly, the Act makes it an offence:

"if any person has in his possession or control—

(a) any live or dead wild bird or any part of, or anything derived from, such a bird; or

(b) an egg of a wild bird or any part of such an egg" (s 1(2)).

It should be noted the section 1(1) offence uses the word "intentionally". It is not an offence that can be committed by mistake, for example by accidentally striking a wild bird with a motor vehicle. If, however, the offending act is deliberate, liability is strict. It is no defence that the accused did not know that the bird was wild (*Kirkland* v *Robinson* [1987] Crim LR 643).

The section 1(2) offence involves "possession or control" of the bird or egg. These words have caused difficulty in criminal law from time to time, but in this context it will normally be pretty obvious whether there is possession or control. If doubt should arise in any instance useful guidance can be found in the House of Lords decision, *Warner* v *Metropolitan Police Commissioner* [1969] 2 AC 256, a case under the Drugs (Prevention of Misuse) Act 1964 which reviewed much of the case law.

A person shall not be guilty of the offence of having possession or control, however, if he shows that the bird or egg had not been killed or taken in contravention of the Act, or of the previous legislation (the Protection of Birds Acts 1954–1967, now repealed) or orders made under the legislation. Nor shall he be guilty if he shows that the bird, egg, bits and pieces or derivatives of them in his possession or control had been sold (whether to him or to any other person) otherwise than in contravention of the legislation (s 1(3)). Taking gulls' eggs, or, before 15 April in any year, lapwings' eggs, for food may be permitted by official licences (s 16(2)(b)).

The burden of proving these defences falls on the defendant. It will not be the criminal burden of proof beyond reasonable doubt, but the less onerous burden of proof on a balance of probabilities, as can be seen from analogous instances such as *R v Hudson* [1966] 1 QB 448 (CCA) under the Mental Health Act 1959.

There are other exceptions and defences to the 1981 Act offences that we shall examine later. First, the meaning given to some of the key words is important.

2. Definitions

(a) "Wild bird"

A wild bird is defined in section 27(1) to mean "any bird of a kind which is ordinarily resident in or is a visitor to Great Britain in a wild state but does not include poultry". Nor does it include any game bird except for the purposes of section 5 (prohibiting certain methods of killing or taking wild birds) and section 16 (permitting certain activities under official licences). Any bird "shown to have been bred in captivity" is not a wild bird (s 1(6)), and the Act says that a bird shall not be treated as bred in captivity "unless its parents were lawfully in captivity when the egg was laid" (s 27(2)).

(b) "Poultry"

"Poultry" (excluded from the definition of wild bird) means domestic fowls, geese, ducks, guinea-fowls, pigeons, quails and turkeys (s 27(1)).

(c) "Game bird"

Few expressions in English statutes have such a variety of meanings as "game". It is just as well, therefore, that the 1981 Act gives its own definition of "game bird". It means here "any pheasant, partridge, grouse (or moor game), black (or heath) game or ptarmigan" (s 27(1)).

(d) "Destroy"

In relation to an egg, "destroy" includes doing anything to the egg which is calculated to prevent it hatching (s 27(1)). The practice by a small minority of gamekeepers of pricking the eggs of predators is therefore illegal.

3. Birds protected by a special penalty

Rarer or more vulnerable species are given special protection by the 1981 Act. They are listed in Schedule 1 to the Act. "A special penalty" (a higher fine, see p 121 below) is laid down for committing either of the two basic offences in respect of these birds (s 1(4)). Then two additional offences are created to protect these rarer birds.

(a) Disturbing nesting Schedule 1 birds and young

It is an offence:

"if any person intentionally—

(a) disturbs any wild bird included in Schedule 1 while it is building a nest or is in, on or near a nest containing eggs or young; or

(b) disturbs dependent young of such a bird" (s 1(5)).

The special penalty also attaches to these two offences.

Schedule 1 is in two parts. The birds in Part I are protected by the special penalty at all times. The few in Part II are protected by the special penalty only during their close season (from the beginning of February to the end of August, s 2(4)). The two basic offences and the two additional offences mentioned above apply to birds in Part II outside the close season, but the special penalty arises only where offences are committed during the close season.

The schedule is set out here giving only the common English names of the birds. The Act also gives their scientific Latin names. The schedule has not been varied since enactment.

SCHEDULE 1

BIRDS WHICH ARE PROTECTED BY SPECIAL PENALTIES

PART I

At all times

Avocet	Corncrake
Bee-eater	Crake, Spotted
Bittern	Crossbills (all species)
Bittern, Little	Curlew, Stone
Bluethroat	Divers (all species)
Brambling	Dotterel
Bunting, Cirl	Duck, Long-tailed
Bunting, Lapland	Eagle, Golden
Bunting, Snow	Eagle, White-tailed
Buzzard, Honey	Falcon, Gyr
Chough	Fieldfare

Firecrest
Garganey
Godwit, Black-tailed
Goshawk
Grebe, Black-necked
Grebe, Slavonian
Greenshank
Gull, Little
Gull, Mediterranean
Harriers (all species)
Heron, Purple
Hobby
Hoopoe
Kingfisher
Kite, Red
Merlin
Oriole, Golden
Osprey
Owl, Barn
Owl, Snowy
Peregrine
Petrel, Leach's
Phalarope, Red-necked
Plover, Kentish
Plover, Little Ringed
Quail, Common
Redstart, Black
Redwing
Rosefinch, Scarlet

Ruff
Sandpiper, Green
Sandpiper, Purple
Sandpiper, Wood
Scaup
Scoter, Common
Scoter, Velvet
Serin
Shorelark
Shrike, Red-backed
Spoonbill
Stilt, Black-winged
Stint, Temminck's
Swan, Bewick's
Swan, Whooper
Tern, Black
Tern, Little
Tern, Roseate
Tit, Bearded
Tit, Crested
Treecreeper, Short-toed
Warbler, Cetti's
Warbler, Dartford
Warbler, Marsh
Warbler, Savi's
Whimbrel
Woodlark
Wryneck

PART II

During the close season

Goldeneye
Goose, Greylag (in Outer Hebrides, Caithness, Sutherland and Wester
        Ross only)
Pintail

4. Close season protection

Whilst the 1981 Act gives special protection to the birds listed in Schedule 1, less than the basic protection is given to other lists of birds. They are in Schedule 2. Schedule 2 is set out below. Again the schedule has two parts. It is not an offence to kill or take any bird listed in Part I of Schedule 2, or to injure it in an attempt to kill it, outside the close season for the bird in question (s 2(1)). These are all game birds and wildfowl, none of them, of course, rare.

(a) Close seasons

The usual close season begins on 1 February and ends on 31 August; but not the close season for capercaillie and woodcock which begins on 1 February and ends on 30 September; for snipe it is 1 February to 11 August; and for wild duck and wild geese in or over any area below high water mark of ordinary spring tides, it is 21 February to 31 August (s 2(4)). In each instance the whole of both dates mentioned is in the close season.

The Secretary of State can, by order, vary the close season for any wild bird with respect to the whole or any part of Great Britain (s 2(5)). He may also make temporary orders giving special protection outside the close season, up to 14 days at a time, for birds in Part II of Schedule 1 and Part I of Schedule 2 (s 2(6)). This has been done at times when wildfowl have been especially vulnerable because of exceptionally frosty weather.

(b) Sundays and Christmas Day

In Scotland the birds in Schedule 2 may not be killed or taken on Sundays or on Christmas Day—a law deriving from a solicitude for people's souls, rather than for the birds. The 1981 Act has no such Sunday ban for England and Wales, though the Secretary of State has power to impose one, by order, for specified areas (s 2(3)).

5. Rights of "authorised persons"

The second part of Schedule 2 to the 1981 Act makes provision for a list of birds which may be killed or taken at all times by a category known to the Act as "authorised persons". Authorised persons under the 1981 Act are owners and occupiers of the land, holders of sporting rights and anyone authorised by them or authorised in writing by the local authority, or by any of the Nature Conservancy Councils, a district fishery board in Scotland, a local sea fisheries committee, the National Rivers Authority or a sewerage undertaker. This appears from the definition of "authorised person" in section 27(1) of the 1981 Act as amended by the Water Act 1989, and from the definition of "occupier". "Occupier", in relation to any land other than the foreshore, includes any person having a right of hunting, shooting, fishing or taking game or fish (s 27(1)).

Schedule 2 Part II originally listed 13 common birds considered to be pests, at least by farmers and horticulturists. All have been removed by SI 1992 No 3010. An "authorised person" shall not be guilty of either of the two basic offences referred to above by—

(a) killing or taking a bird included in Part II of Schedule 2, or injuring such a bird in the course of an attempt to kill it;

(b) taking, damaging or destroying a nest of such a bird; or

(c) taking, damaging or destroying an egg of such a bird (s 2(2)).

Even in an area of special protection under section 3 of the 1981 Act (see below) authorised persons may with impunity take or kill this list of birds, take, damage or destroy their nests or eggs, and disturb them and dependent young when nesting (s 3(2)). There are further exemptions from criminal liability for authorised persons among the exceptions set out in section 4 of the 1981 Act (see p 105 below).

Schedule 2 to the 1981 Act is here set out as enacted, but giving the common English names of the species only.

SCHEDULE 2

BIRDS WHICH MAY BE KILLED OR TAKEN

PART I

Outside the close season

Capercaillie	Mallard
Coot	Moorhen
Duck, Tufted	Pintail
Gadwall	Plover, Golden
Goldeneye	Pochard
Goose, Canada	Shoveler
Goose, Greylag	Snipe, Common
Goose, Pink-footed	Teal
Goose, White-fronted (in	Wigeon
England and Wales only)	Woodcock

PART II*

By authorised persons at all times

Crow	Magpie
Dove, Collared	Pigeon, Feral
Gull, Great Black-backed	Rook
Gull, Lesser Black-backed	Sparrow, House
Gull, Herring	Starling
Jackdaw	Woodpigeon
Jay	

*It should be noted that Part II presently contains no birds; all have been removed by SI 1992 No 3010.

6. Areas of special protection

The Secretary of State is given power by the 1981 Act to specify, by orders, "areas of special protection" for wild birds (s 3). About 40 exist. The scope is limited because designation requires the co-operation of the owners and occupiers of the land, and the section itself states that the making of an order "shall not affect the exercise by any person of any right vested in him, whether as owner, lessee or occupier of any land in that area or by virtue of a licence or agreement". Areas of special protection are therefore mainly to control the conduct of people entering with no title to access. It must be remembered that it is the landowners and occupiers who often have the primary interest in conservation, and who welcome the helpful hand of the law in protecting wildlife, especially when the site has been purchased to be a reserve, for example by the Royal Society for the Protection of Birds.

Orders under section 3 can extend the full protection that the 1981 Act gives birds in Schedule 1 to all, or to specified, wild birds in the area of special protection, and to their nests, eggs and young. It can be made an offence in these areas to disturb any specified species while it is building a nest, or while it is in, on or near a nest containing young; or to disturb dependent young of such a bird. The order can make it an offence to enter the area of special protection, or any part of it, either at any time or at specified times. Offences committed under the Act in the area can be made subject to a special penalty.

Before the Secretary of State may make an order for an area of special protection, he is required to give particulars in writing of the intended order to every owner and occupier of any land to be included. Where in his opinion it is impracticable to give direct notice—for instance if they cannot be readily traced, or they are too numerous—he may place an advertisement in a newspaper circulating in the district. He can then only make the order if all the owners and occupiers consent, or if there are no outstanding objections from any of them three months after notice has been given or the advertisement published.

7. Exceptions to criminal liability

If criminal laws are too rigid, they lead to injustices and inhibit enforcement. Exceptions and defences to criminal offences are therefore nearly always laid down. In the case of the offences concerning wild birds there are general exceptions, and there are also exceptions which apply only to "authorised persons".

(a) General exceptions

Exceptions to the two basic offences described above, and to anything made unlawful (by orders) in areas of special protection, are provided by section 4(1) and (2) of the 1981 Act. The offences will not be committed in the following instances.

Official pest, weed and disease control: Anything done in pursuance of a requirement by the Minister of Agriculture, Fisheries and Food, or the Secretary of State under section 98 of the Agriculture Act (which deals with pest and weed control), or an order under sections 21 or 22 of the Animal Health Act 1981 (which deals with control of disease) shall not be an offence under section 1 or a section 3 order (s 4(1)(a), (b)). Nor will anything done pursuant to orders under any other provision of the Animal Health Act 1981, except in the case of a wild bird included in Schedule 1 to the 1981 Act (the rarer birds) or the nest or egg of such a bird (s 4(1)(c)).

Disabled birds: Taking a wild bird by a person "if he shows that the bird had been disabled otherwise than by his unlawful act and was taken solely for the purpose of tending it and releasing it when no longer disabled"; and "the killing of any wild bird if he shows that the bird had been so seriously disabled otherwise than by his unlawful act that there was no reasonable chance of its recovering" shall not be offences (s 4(2)(a), (b)).

The burden of proving the defence will fall to the defendant, but, as we saw with regard to section 1(3) above on an analogy with the likes of *R* v *Hudson* [1966] 1 QB 488, it will not need to be proved beyond reasonable doubt, but simply on a balance of probabilities. Anyone taking care of a disabled bird would be wise to obtain expert advice, for example from the RSPB, before releasing it to the wild again.

Lawful operations: A person will also have a defence for any act that he shows was "the incidental result of a lawful operation and could not reasonably have been avoided" (s 4(2)(c)). It would appear from this wording that the defence does not turn on whether the lawful act was reasonable, but whether in doing it the incidental result could reasonably have been avoided. The distinction is important, particularly for farmers. If, for example, a nest or eggs of a ground-nesting bird were destroyed when a field was harrowed, it would not be open to a prosecutor to contend that it was unreasonable to harrow the field, but the accused farmer would need to show that in harrowing it he could not reasonably have safeguarded the nest or eggs. Again the burden of proving the defence will be on a balance of probabilities.

Defences to "possession or control" offences: The defences in section 1(3) of the 1981 Act have been noted above.

Acting under licence: Acts which would otherwise be offences under the 1981 Act can be carried out lawfully if officially authorised by licence. As licensing may also apply to animals and plants, and the provisions are complex, the subject is dealt with separately at pp 120-121 below.

(b) Exceptions for "authorised persons"

An "authorised person" (defined at p 102 above) shall not be guilty of either of the two basic offences, or of anything made unlawful by order in an area of special protection, by killing or injuring any wild bird, other than a bird listed in Schedule 1 (the rarer birds)

"If he shows that his action was necessary for the purpose of—

(a)   preserving public health or public or air safety;

(b)   preventing the spread of disease; or

(c)   preventing serious damage to livestock, foodstuffs for livestock, crops, vegetables, fruit, growing timber, or fisheries" (s 4(3)).

Fisheries and fish farms: Protecting fisheries and fish farms against the depredations of herons and cormorants can be a knotty problem. Attempting to kill the predators is often an inadequate solution. The RSPB, the Ministry of Agriculture, Fisheries and Food ("MAFF"), the National Rivers Authority, the National Farmers' Union and the Country Landowners' Association can advise on alternative measures.

8. Unlawful methods of taking and killing wild birds

Whilst the 1981 Act permits the normal exercise of sporting rights, it outlaws not only killing or taking the rarer wild birds, but also methods considered cruel or unsporting. Section 5 of the Act contains a catalogue of prohibited methods. They can only lawfully be employed, if at all, under official licences (see p 120 below). The references to section 5 below are to the section as amended by the Wildlife and Countryside (Amendment) Act 1991.

(a) Setting unlawful articles in position

It is an offence to set in position any of a list of articles "of such a nature and so placed as to be calculated to cause bodily injury to any wild bird coming into contact therewith". The list is: "any springe, trap, gin, snare, hook and line, any electrical device for killing, stunning or frightening or any poisonous, poisoned or stupefying substance" (s 5(1)(a)).

(b) Unlawful devices

It is an offence to use for killing or taking a wild bird any of the above list of articles, or a net, baited board, bird-lime or substance of a like nature, bow or crossbow, explosive (other than ammunition for a firearm), automatic or semi-automatic weapon, a shot gun having a muzzle more than one and three-quarter inches in diameter, device for illuminating a target, sighting device for night shooting, artificial lighting or mirror or other dazzling device, gas or smoke, or chemical wetting agent (s 5(1)(b), (c)). "Firearm" has the same meaning as in the Firearms Act 1968 (s 27(1) of the 1981 Act).

(c) Unlawful decoys

It is an offence to use as a decoy for killing or taking any wild bird, a sound recording, or any live bird or animal which is tethered or secured by braces or similar appliances, or is blind, maimed or injured (s 5(1)(d)).

(d) Vehicles

It is an offence to use any mechanically propelled vehicle in immediate pursuit of a wild bird for the purpose of killing or taking it (s 5(1)(e)). A wide meaning is given to "vehicle". It includes aircraft, hovercraft and boats (s 27(1)).

(e) Causing or permitting the use of unlawful methods

It is an offence knowingly to cause or permit the use of any of the unlawful methods under section 5 of the 1981 Act, set out above (s 5(1)(f)). This was added by the Wildlife and Countryside (Amendment) Act 1991 to ensure that an employer, or anyone else giving the orders, who may well be the principal culprit, could be prosecuted as well as, or instead of, the person committing the illegal act.

(f) Special penalty

All the offences under section 5 carry a "special penalty" on conviction (see p 121 below).

(g) Exceptions and defences

It is a defence to a charge of unlawfully setting an article in position under section 5(1)(a) to show that it was done for the purpose of killing or taking, in the interests of public health, agriculture, forestry, fisheries or nature conservation, a wild animal which could lawfully be taken by that means, provided that all reasonable precautions were taken to prevent injury to wild birds (s 5(4), (4A)).

In spite of the ban on nets and traps, it is lawful for an "authorised person" (defined above) to use a cage-trap or net to take a bird listed in Schedule 2 Part II (the pestilential birds); and to take wild duck in a duck decoy, provided that it was in use before the passing of the Protection of Birds Act 1954; and to use a cage-trap or net for taking a game bird solely for the purpose of breeding. As an exception to the exceptions, in no case will it be lawful to use a net to take a bird in flight, or to take a bird on the ground by means of a net projected or propelled otherwise than by hand (s 5(5)).

(h) Poisoning and pesticides

The irresponsible practice by a small minority of gamekeepers and farmers of laying out poison baits to kill predators is dangerous and illegal. It takes such a toll of raptors, livestock, pets, honey bees and animals in the wild, that a well-organised joint campaign of government and voluntary bodies operates with the aim of stamping out illegal poisoning and advising on lawful pest control. Golden eagles, red kites and barn owls, among other rare or threatened species, constantly figure as victims of poisoning, usually from baits laced with illegal pesticides left in open country, according to the annual reports of the Environmental Panel of the Advisory Committee on Pesticides, which make melancholy reading.

The placing of baits calculated to poison wild birds is an offence under section 5(1)(a) of the 1981 Act (see p 106 above), and the law has been strengthened by Part III of the Food and Environment Protection Act 1985 and the Control of Pesticide Regulations 1986 (SI 1986 No 1510) made under it. The use of pesticides, their storage, advertisement, sale and supply are regulated by these measures. Pesticides include a range of poisonous substances, such as fungicides, insecticides and herbicides. Only approved pesticides may be used, and only in a manner for which consent has been given.

Pesticides can, of course, accidentally pollute and poison, and MAFF and the Health and Safety Executive have issued a Code of Practice for the Safe Use of Pesticides on Farms and Holdings. MAFF also issued a code in 1984 on disposal of unwanted pesticides and containers.

MAFF operates a Wildlife Incident Investigation Scheme to examine suspected poisonings, and initiates prosecutions. The Department for Agriculture and Fisheries operates a similar scheme in Scotland. MAFF advises farmers and others on responsible pest control and issues booklets advising what to do if anyone discovers a poison bait or a suspected incident of poisoning. The Regional Wildlife and Storage Biologist at the MAFF regional office should immediately be consulted, or MAFF's Central Science Laboratory at Block C, Hook Rise South, Tolworth, Surbiton, KT6 7NF. Telephone 081–330 8239. A free telephone line, open between 9 am and 5 pm, can be used on 0800–321 600.

9. Trading in wild birds

The provisions in the 1981 Act against trading in live and dead wild birds are a useful deterrent, but in spite of the breadth of the possession offences in section 1(2) of the Act (see Two basic offences, p 98) and the publicity given to criminal prosecutions, a black market trade continues, particularly in the eggs and carcasses of rare birds, encouraged by high prices offered by collectors. Offences in section 6 of the Act aim to tackle the problem.

(a) Sales and advertising

It is an offence if any person sells, offers or exposes for sale, or has in his possession for sale any live wild bird (s 6(1)(a)), dead wild bird, or part of one or "anything derived from" a wild bird (s 6(2)(a)), or any egg or part of an egg of a wild bird (s 6(1)(a)); or advertises such trading (ss 6(1)(b), 6(2)(b)).

(b) Permitted trading

As an exception in the case of *live* birds, the offence is not committed if the bird has been ringed or marked in accordance with regulations made by the Secretary of State and is of a species listed in Part I of Schedule 3 to the 1981 Act (s 6(5)). The Wildlife and Countryside (Registration and Ringing of Certain Captive Birds) Regulations 1982, SI 1982 No 1221 (amended by SI 1991 No 478), have been made under this subsection. As an exception in the case of *dead* birds, no offence is committed if the bird is of a species listed in Part II of Schedule 3 (there is only one at present—woodpigeons), or, between 1 September and the following 28 February (both days included) is a bird included in Part III of Schedule 3 (s 6(6)). Schedule 3 is here set out as enacted, but giving only the English common names of the species. This schedule has been varied by SI 1992 No 3010, which removed Feral Pigeon from Part II.

SCHEDULE 3

BIRDS WHICH MAY BE SOLD

PART I

Alive at all times if ringed and bred in captivity

Blackbird	Linnet
Brambling	Magpie
Bullfinch	Owl, Barn
Bunting, Reed	Redpoll
Chaffinch	Siskin
Dunnock	Starling
Goldfinch	Thrush, Song
Greenfinch	Twite
Jackdaw	Yellowhammer
Jay	

PART II

Dead at all times

Pigeon, Feral	Woodpigeon

PART III

Dead from 1 September to 28 February

Capercaillie	Pochard
Coot	Shoveler
Duck, Tufted	Snipe, Common
Mallard	Teal
Pintail	Wigeon
Plover, Golden	Woodcock

(c) Registration

Section 6 makes an exception to the trading offences with regard to dead birds, their bits and pieces, for persons registered under regulations made by the Secretary of State, though breach of the registration regulations is an offence (s 6(8)). Provision is made for disqualifying offenders from registration, and for authorised officials to enter and inspect premises where a registered person keeps any wild birds, to ascertain whether an offence is being, or has been committed (s 6(8), (9)). It is an offence intentionally to obstruct any person exercising the power (s 6(10)). From the decision of Lord Goddard CJ under the licensing laws in *Hinchcliffe* v *Seldon* [1955] 3 All ER 406, it seems that a deliberate hindrance short of violence is an obstruction.

10. Birds in captivity

The 1981 Act lists in Schedule 4 birds for which it is an offence carrying a special penalty to have possession or control of unless they are registered, ringed and marked in accordance with regulations. There are special penal provisions against previous offenders under the Act (s 7). As in section 6 (see above) provision is made for entry and inspection of premises where Schedule 4 birds are kept (s 7(6)), and it is an offence intentionally to obstruct any person exercising the power. Schedule 4 is not reproduced here. It is a long list of species similar to Schedule 1 Part I, set out above.

The 1981 Act contains provisions for the humane treatment of captive birds (s 8) and a ban on showing birds for competitions (s 6(3)).

11. Swans

Swans hold a privileged position in the hierarchy of British birds. They are "fowl royal" and in the main belong to the Crown, though swans on private waters not having the royal mark belong to the landowners (*Case of Swans* (1592) [1558–1774] All ER Rep 641). Swan-upping to mark the beaks of swans is a regular occurrence. Native swans in the UK therefore enjoy unique protection. Swans have been the victims of lead poisoning, but the risk has been greatly reduced since anglers some years ago ceased to use lead shot and weights (other than "dust shot"). Their supply and importation have been banned by regulations made under the Control of Pollution Act 1974, s 100 (Control of Pollution (Anglers' Lead Weights) Regulations 1986 (SI 1986 No 1992)).

B. Animals in the wild

The 1981 Act uses a similar approach to protect wild animals as it does for wild birds. It contains similar criminal offences and provides similar defences, but it is not so sweeping as regards the creatures protected. With regard to birds, the Act starts from the position of protecting *all* wild birds, and then makes qualifications and exceptions. In the case of animals, a selected list only (set out in Sch 5) is protected, though the devices and methods declared unlawful are outlawed whatever the animal targeted. Commentary on the provisions is not repeated where the provisions for wild animals are akin to those for wild birds.

1. Protected wild animals

The creatures listed as protected animals in Schedule 5 to the 1981 Act include insects, reptiles and even fish.

"Wild animal" is defined to mean "any animal (other than a bird) which is or (before it was killed or taken) was living wild" (s 27(1)). Animals born and kept in captivity are therefore excluded. Where the Act refers to an animal, an egg, larva, pupa or other immature stage of an animal is included, unless the context otherwise requires (s 27(3)).

Schedule 5 is here set out as amended by the orders referred to on p 97 (save for SI 1992 No 2350), but giving the common English names only of the species.

SCHEDULE 5

ANIMALS WHICH ARE PROTECTED

Adder*
Anemone, Ivell's Sea
Anemone, Startlet Sea
Apus
Bats, Horseshoe (all species)
Bats, Typical (all species)
Beetle, Rainbow Leaf
Beetle, Violet Click
Burbot
Butterflies:
  Northern Brown Angus
  Adonis Blue
  Chalkhill Blue
  Large Blue
  Silver-studded Blue
  Small Blue
  Large Copper
  Purple Emperor
  Duke of Burgundy Fritillary
  Heath, Fritillary
  Glanville Fritillary
  High Brown Fritillary
  Black Hairstreak
  Large Heath
  Mountain Ringlet
  Chequered Skipper
  Lulworth Skipper
  Silver Spotted Skipper
  Swallowtail
  Large Tortoiseshell
  Wood White
Cat, Wild
Cicada, New Forest
Crayfish, Atlantic Stream
Cricket, Field

Cricket, Mole
Dormouse
Dolphins (all)
Dragonfly, Norfolk Aeshna
Frog, Common*
Grasshopper, Wart-biter
Leech, Medicinal
Lizard, Sand
Lizard, Viviparous
Marten, Pine
Mat, Trembling Sea
Moths:
  Barberry Carpet
  Black-veined
  Essex Emerald
  New Forest Burnet
  Reddish Buff
  Viper's Buglon
Mussel, Freshwater Pearl
Newt, Great Crested (otherwise
  known as Wart newt)
Newt, Palmate*
Newt, Smooth*
Otter, Common
Porpoises (all)
Sandworm, Lagoon
Shad, Allis
Shrimp, Fairy
Shrimp, Lagoon Sand
Slow-worm*
Snail, Glutinous
Snail, Sandbowl
Snake, Grass*
Snake, Smooth
Spider, Fen Raft

111

Spider, Ladybird	Vendace
Squirrel, Red	Walrus
Toad, Common*	Whales (all)
Toad, Natterjack	Whitefish
Turtles, Marine (all)	

* The creatures marked with an asterisk are protected by some only of the offences referred to below.

SI 1992 No 2350 added five more Beetles, three Snails, Northern Hatchet Shell, Sussex Emerald Moth, Pink Sea Fan, Lagoon Sea Slug and Sturgeon to Schedule 5.

2. The offences

In any proceedings for the offences of killing, taking, injuring, possessing and trading in wild animals and using prohibited methods for killing and taking wild animals, the 1981 Act states that "the animal in question shall be presumed to have been a wild animal unless the contrary is shown" (ss 9(6) and 11(5), (7)). The burden of proving the contrary is therefore thrown on the defendant.

(a) Kills, injures or takes

It is an offence "if any person intentionally kills, injures or takes any wild animal included in Schedule 5" (s 9(1)). The importance of the word "intentionally" is noted on p 98 above with regard to the equivalent offence concerning wild birds.

(b) Possession or control

"If any person has in his possession or control any live or dead wild animal included in Schedule 5 or any part of, or anything derived from, such an animal", he commits an offence (s 9(2)). Such a person has a defence to this offence, however, if it is shown that the animal had not been killed or taken contrary to the 1981 Act or the Wild Creatures and Wild Plants Act 1975, or that the animal, or bits and pieces, or derivatives, in his possession or control had been sold (whether to him or any other person) otherwise than in contravention of those provisions (s 9(3)).

(c) Interference with an animal's shelter

Akin to the offences of interfering with nests and with breeding wild birds, it is an offence:

"if any person intentionally—
(a) damages or destroys, or obstructs access to, any structure or place which any wild animal included in Schedule 5 uses for shelter or protection; or

(b) disturbs any such animal while it is occupying a structure or place which it uses for that purpose" (s 9(4)).

Anything done within a dwellinghouse will not be an offence under these provisions (s 10(2)), but there is a special, though rather strange provision, regarding bats.

(d) Bats

In the case of the bats listed in Schedule 5, the dwellinghouse defence is limited to anything done "in the living area of the dwellinghouse", unless the Nature Conservancy Council for the area is previously notified of the proposed action or operation and is allowed a reasonable time to advise whether it should be carried out, and, if so, by what method. The requirement to notify the Conservancy Council also applies to the defence of an incidental result of a lawful operation mentioned below (s 10(5) as amended by the Environmental Protection Act 1990). Bats must not therefore be disturbed in any belfry that a house may have without first notifying the Conservancy Council. An oddity is that the Act does not require the advice to be followed. So long as notification is given, no offence is committed even if the advice is ignored.

(e) Trading offences

There are offences equivalent to those for trading in wild birds: these forbid transactions in live or dead Schedule 5 animals, or parts of or derivatives from them, and advertising (s 9(5)). The substance of the offences is the same as for birds in section 6 (see p 108), but there is no provision in the 1981 Act for registering persons to deal in or keep Schedule 5 animals, and there are no special penalties.

3. General defences and exceptions

The same general defences as those given by section 4(1)(a) and (b) and section 4(2)(a), (b) and (c) concerning wild birds, tailored for animals, are given by the 1981 Act with respect to Schedule 5 animals—that is, exceptions for things required to be done by Ministers or under the Animal Health Act 1981 (s 10(1)), humane acts towards disabled animals (s 10(3)(a), (b)) and unavoidable results of lawful acts (s 10(3)(c)).

(a) "Authorised persons"

"Authorised persons" (as defined on p 102 above to include the landowner and occupier) escape criminal liability for actions necessary to prevent serious damage by Schedule 5 animals "to livestock, foodstuffs for livestock, crops, vegetables, fruit, growing timber or any other form of property or to fisheries" (s 10(4)). The defence cannot be relied on, however, if the need for the action taken was apparent in advance and no licence authorising it had been applied for under section 16 (see p 120

113

below) or "the application for such a licence had been determined" (s 10(6)).

4. Unlawful methods of killing or taking wild animals

Most of the methods and devices outlawed for harming, taking or killing wild birds are also prohibited for wild animals, but there is an important difference. Some of them are unlawful only when targeted at a list of species selected for special protection. These species are listed in Schedule 6 to the 1981 Act (set out below). The intricacies of the prohibitions can be found in section 11 of the 1981 Act as amended by the Wildlife and Countryside (Amendment) Act 1991. In proceedings for an offence, the animal in question shall be presumed to be a wild animal unless the contrary is shown (s 11(5)).

(a) Devices etc against "any wild animal"

It is illegal to set in position a self-locking snare "so placed as to be calculated to cause bodily injury to any wild animal coming into contact with it" (s 11(1)(a)). Other snares may be used to trap animals that are not listed in Schedule 6, but it is an offence if the snares are not inspected at least once a day (s 11(3)). It is, however, an offence to use as a decoy any live mammal or bird whatever for taking or killing any kind of wild animal (s 11(1)(c)).

The use of a self-locking snare, bow, crossbow or explosive (other than ammunition for a firearm) for killing or taking any wild animal is an offence (s 11(1)(b)). It is also an offence to cause or permit the illegal act to be done (s 11)(1)(d)).

(b) Devices etc against Schedule 6 animals

It is an offence to set in position any trap or snare, electrical device for killing or stunning, or any poisonous, poisoned or stupefying substance of a nature and so placed as to be calculated to cause bodily injury to any wild animal listed in Schedule 6 to the 1981 Act (s 11(2)(a)). It is a defence to show that the accused set the article in position in the interests of public health, agriculture, forestry, fisheries or nature conservation, provided that all reasonable precautions were taken to prevent injury to any Schedule 6 animal (s 11(6)).

It is a separate offence to take or kill Schedule 6 animals with these devices, and likewise with any automatic or semi-automatic weapon, device for illuminating a target, sighting device for night shooting, artificial light, mirror or other dazzling device, gas or smoke, any sound recording as a decoy or any mechanically propelled vehicle in immediate pursuit of the animal. It is also an offence to cause or permit the illegal acts to be done (s 11(2)).

Schedule 6 is here set out as enacted, but using only the common English names of the species. The schedule has not been varied since enactment.

SCHEDULE 6

ANIMALS WHICH MAY NOT BE KILLED OR TAKEN BY CERTAIN METHODS

Badger
Bats, Horseshoe (all species)
Bats, Typical (all species)
Cat, Wild
Dolphin, Bottle-nosed
Dolphin, Common
Dormice (all species)
Hedgehog

Marten, Pine
Otter, Common
Polecat
Porpoise, Harbour (otherwise
   known as Common
   Porpoise)
Shrews (all species)
Squirrel, Red

5. Deer

Deer have their own legislation. It has conveniently been consolidated in the Deer Act 1991.

(a) Close seasons

Close seasons are laid down for four species, namely, Red, Fallow, Roe and Sika deer. For stags and bucks the annual close season is from 1 May to 31 July (inclusive), except it is 1 November to 31 March for the buck Roe Deer; for hinds and does it is 1 March to 31 October (Sch 1). It is an offence to take or wilfully kill them in the close season (s 2). The occupier of the land, members of his household or his employees (provided that they have written permission) and any holder of the right to take or kill deer, may lawfully shoot the four species, in the day time, in any season, if the deer are damaging crops, vegetables, fruit, growing timber or any other form of property on cultivated land, pasture or enclosed woodland, provided that the shooting is necessary to prevent serious damage (s 7). The persons given this freedom are called "authorised persons", but it will be noted that the definition is different from that in the 1981 Act.

(b) Poaching offences

Section 1 lays down offences of poachers entering land in search of, or in pursuit of, deer of any species, intentionally killing deer, or attempting to (s 5), and removing a carcass. It is a defence if the accused had authority, or believed he would have consent.

(c) Prohibited weapons and devices

Certain weapons and ammunition are banned for killing or injuring deer, including any smooth bore gun, rifle of less than 0.240 inches calibre or muzzle energy below 1,700 footpounds, air weapons, arrows, spears, missiles containing poisoning or stupefying drugs, and other inhumane

115

or unsporting armoury or devices (s 4). Possession of the proscribed weapons or ammunition for illegal use against deer is also an offence.

(d) Other offences

No deer of any species may be taken or wilfully killed at night (from one hour after sunset to one hour before sunrise) by any person in any season of the year. The Act attempts to close outlets for poachers by confining the lawful dealing in venison to licensed game dealers (s 10).

(e) Defences

Humane acts of various kinds are allowed. It is also a defence if an offending act was in compliance with a requirement of MAFF (s 6). Provision is also made for the nature conservancies to license acts which would otherwise be unlawful (s 8).

6. Badgers

The extent to which the badger has won the hearts of the public is shown by the fact that a number of Acts have been passed over the years for its protection. The Acts are now consolidated in the Protection of Badgers Act 1992.

The Act makes it an offence for a person to kill, injure or take (or attempt to) any badger (s 1(1)); to have possession of, or under his control, a dead badger or any part of, or anything derived from, a dead badger (s 1(3)); or to trade in, or have in his possession, or under his control, a live badger (s 4). The Act has further offences of ill-treatment of badgers; using badger tongs; digging for badgers; using a firearm other than a smooth bore weapon of not less than 20 bore, or a rifle using ammunition having a muzzle energy not less than 160 footpounds and a bullet weighing not less than 30 grains (s 2); and marking, attaching any ring, tag or other marking device to any badger (s 5). It is an offence to interfere with a badger sett by damaging, destroying, obstructing access to, causing a dog to enter, or disturbing a badger occupying it (s 3).

Where a dog is used in, or is present at, the commission of an offence against section 1(1), 2 or 3, the court has power to order "the destruction or other disposal of the dog" and to disqualify the offender from having custody of a dog (s 13).

(a) Exceptions

As in the 1981 Act there are exceptions to criminal liability in the case of humane acts to disabled badgers, unavoidable killing or injuring a badger as an incidental result of a lawful act, and, in respect of the section 1(1) and section 3 offences, actions necessary to prevent serious damage to land, crops, poultry or any other form of property (s 7).

Obstructing setts for the purposes of hunting foxes with hounds is allowed subject to safeguards specified in the Act (s 8).

There is provision for official licensing of acts which would otherwise be offences for a range of purposes scientific or educational, or to do with conservation, preservation, planning, agriculture and forestry, land drainage, controlling foxes and the investigation of offences (s 10).

Where a constable reasonably suspects an offence under the Protection of Badgers Act 1992, he has power to stop and search persons, vehicles and articles, and seize and detain anything liable to be forfeited on conviction (s 11)—namely, any badger, badger skin, or weapon or article used in committing the offence (s 12(4)).

7. Seals

Seals in the wild are protected by the Conservation of Seals Act 1970. The Act makes it an offence to use poison for taking or killing a seal, or any firearm, other than a rifle using ammunition of at least 600 footpounds muzzle energy and a bullet weighing at least 45 grains (s 1); and lays down annual close seasons for grey seals, from 1 September to 31 December inclusive, and for common seals, from 1 June to 31 August inclusive (s 2). It is lawful to take a disabled seal with the intention of tending and releasing it; and unavoidable killing or injuring a seal incidental to a lawful act is a defence to the offences, as is killing a seal which is causing damage to a fishing net or fishing tackle (s 9). The Act provides for licensing the killing or taking of seals for scientific or educational purposes; zoological gardens or collections; protection of fisheries; managed culling; or the protection of fauna and flora (s 10).

There is also legislation to give effect to international agreements to protect seals, sea otters and whales.

C. Plants in the wild

The 1981 Act follows a simpler plan for the protection of wild plants than its provisions for wild birds and animals, but it is along the same broad lines. Protection is again by meting out criminal liability for damaging activities. A distinction is made between picking and the more lethal uprooting of plants. All wild plants are given some protection against uprooting. A selected list of rarer species (contained in Sch 8, set out below) is given special protection. "Authorised persons" are given more leeway than others.

1. Meaning of "wild plant"

"Wild plant" is defined to mean "any plant which is or (before it was picked, uprooted or destroyed) was growing wild and is of a kind which ordinarily grows in Great Britain in a wild state" (s 27(1)).

2. The offences

(a) Picking and uprooting

It is an offence:

"If any person—

(a) intentionally picks, uproots or destroys any wild plant included in Schedule 8; or

(b) not being an authorised person, intentionally uproots any wild plant not included in that Schedule" (s 13(1)).

The meaning of "authorised person" is the same as for the wild birds laws (see p 102). It includes the owner and occupier of the land.

The Act repeats here the defence we have already seen for wild birds and animals, that the act was an incidental result of a lawful operation and could not have been reasonably avoided. It is, of course, open to the Nature Conservancy Councils to protect appropriate sites against lawful operations by designating them as sites of special scientific interest.

(b) Trading in wild plants

It is an offence:

"if any person—

(a) sells, offers or exposes for sale, or has in his possession or transports for the purposes of sale, any live or dead wild plant included in Schedule 8, or any part of, or anything derived from, such a plant; or

(b) publishes or causes to be published any advertisement likely to be understood as conveying that he buys or sells, or intends to buy or sell, any of those things" (s 13(2)).

In any proceedings for the offence in (a) the plant shall be presumed to have been wild unless the contrary is shown. The burden is therefore thrown on the accused to prove the contrary on a balance of probabilities.

Schedule 8 is set out here as added to by SI 1988 No 288 referred to on p 97, but giving the common English names of the species only.

SCHEDULE 8

PLANTS WHICH ARE PROTECTED

Adder's Tongue, Least	Calamint, Wood
Alison, Small	Catchfly, Alpine
Broomrape, Bedstraw	Cinquefoil, Rock
Broomrape, Oxtongue	Club-rush, Triangular
Broomrape, Thistle	Coltsfoot, Purple
Cabbage, Lundy	Cotoneaster, Wild

Cottongrass, Slender
Cow-wheat, Field
Crocus, Sand
Cudweed, Jersey
Cudweed, Red-tipped
Diapensia
Eryngo, Field
Fern, Dickie's Bladder
Fern, Killarney
Fleabane, Alpine
Fleabane, Small
Galingale, Brown
Gentian, Alpine
Gentian, Fringed
Gentian, Spring
Germander, Cut-leaved
Germander, Water
Gladiolus, Wild
Goosefoot, Stinking
Grass-poly
Hare's-ear, Sickle-leaved
Hare's-ear, Small
Hawksbeard, Stinking
Heath, Blue
Helleborine, Red
Helleborine, Young's
Horsetail, Branched
Hound's-tongue, Green
Knawel, Perennial
Knotgrass, Sea
Lady's-slipper
Leek, Round-headed
Lettuce, Least
Lily, Snowdon
Marsh-mallow, Rough
Marshwort, Creeping
Milkparsley, Cambridge
Naiad, Holly-leaved
Orchid, Early Spider

Orchid, Fen
Orchid, Ghost
Orchid, Late Spider
Orchid, Lizard
Orchid, Military
Orchid, Monkey
Pear, Plymouth
Pennyroyal
Pigmyweed
Pink, Cheddar
Pink, Childling
Ragwort, Fen
Ramping-fumitory, Martin's
Restharrow, Small
Rockcress, Alpine
Rockcress, Bristol
Sandwort, Norwegian
Sandwort, Teesdale
Saxifrage, Drooping
Saxifrage, Tufted
Solomon's-seal, Whorled
Sow-thistle, Alpine
Spearwort, Adder's-tongue
Speedwell, Fingered
Speedwell, Spiked
Starfruit
Star of Bethlehem, Early
Stonewort, Foxtail
Strapwort
Violet, Fen
Viper's-grass
Water-plaintain, Ribbon Leaved
Wood-sedge, Starved
Woodsia, Alpine
Woodsia, Oblong
Wormwood, Field
Woundwort, Downy
Woundwort, Limestone
Yellow-rattle, Greater

SI 1992 No 2350 added a further seventy-eight plants to Schedule 8, and removed from the list three, namely, two kinds of Sea Lavender and Purple Spurge.

D. Other provisions of Part I of the 1981 Act

1. Species which must not be introduced

Harm can be done to native wildlife in the countryside by introducing into the wild new species of animals or plants, or species of which there are already too many. Harm has been done in modern times by the release, or escape, of imported mink, signal crayfish, polecats, Asian ring-necked parakeets and coypu, to name but a few. The 1981 Act attempts a measure of control by making it an offence to release or allow to escape into the wild any animal of a kind not ordinarily resident, and not a regular visitor to Great Britain in a wild state. There is a similar ban regarding a list of animals set out in Part I of Schedule 9 to the Act (s 14(1)). These are already established in the wild. It is a considerable list of "animals", including birds, fish and reptiles. SI 1992 No 320 added to it three kinds of Crayfish, Sika Deer, New Zealand Flatworm, Italian Crested Newt and Aesculapian Snake; and Barn Owl was added by SI 1992 No 2674.

The Import of Live Fish (England and Wales) Act 1980 furthers this policy (see p 124 below).

To plant or cause to grow in the wild any plant in Part II of Schedule 9 is an offence (s 14(2)). Until 1992 there were only four—Giant Hogweed, Giant Kelp, Japanese Knotweed and Japanese Seaweed. SI 1992 No 320 added four Kelps, three Seaweeds, Green Seafingers and Wakame.

No offence is committed under section 14 by acts authorised in official licences (s 16(4)). It is a defence to a charge under section 14(1) or (2) "to prove that the accused took all reasonable steps and exercised all due diligence to avoid committing the offence" (s 14(3)).

(a) Requirement of seven days' notice

If the accused alleges that the offence was due to the act or default of someone else, he may not rely on the defence (without leave of the court) unless he serves notice on the prosecutor seven clear days before the hearing identifying the other person as best he can (s 14(4)).

2. Official licences

In a fair number of instances, activities which would otherwise be offences under the 1981 Act and the legislation for deer, badgers and seals, may be lawfully performed if done under a licence granted by "the appropriate authority". The appropriate authority is variously the Secretary of State for the Environment, an agriculture Minister or the relevant Nature Conservancy Council (s 16(9)). As with so much in the 1981 Act, the provisions are somewhat complex. They can be found in section 16 and will not be described here in detail. The kinds of activities which may be licensed include anything done for the purposes of science or education; conservation of birds; ringing or marking birds; falconry or aviculture;

photography; taxidermy; collections of birds, plants or animals; preventing the spread of disease; and, the familiar refrain, "preventing serious damage to livestock, foodstuffs for livestock, crops, vegetables, fruit, growing timber or fisheries". English Nature and the Countryside Council for Wales give helpful guidance about the grant of licences.

3. Enforcement of the criminal law and penalties

(a) Powers of constables and occupiers

A constable who has reasonable cause to suspect that a person is committing or has committed an offence under the 1981 Act may without a warrant stop and search the suspect and examine anything he is using or has on him, provided that he has reasonable cause to believe that evidence is to be found. He may seize for production in court any evidence he finds and anything that a court might order to be forfeited. He may arrest the suspect if he fails to give his name and address. The constable may enter any land to do these things, but not, without a warrant, a dwellinghouse (s 19).

Owners and occupiers should not arrest suspects, but they can always require trespassers to leave the land. If a trespasser refuses, he may be removed by the use of no more force than is reasonably necessary. It is a remedy best avoided. If done it should be only as a last resort and with the utmost discretion. Under the Protection of Badgers Act 1992, the landowner, occupier or an employee (as well as a constable) can require anyone committing an offence under the Act to give his name and address and to quit the land. Refusal to do either is a further offence.

(b) Prosecutions

Prosecutions are taken in the magistrates' courts. Local authorities are expressly given the right to institute proceedings for offences (s 25(2)). As well as official prosecutions by the police or authorities, it is open to organisations and individuals to take private prosecutions.

(c) Penalties

Section 21 of the 1981 Act lays down the penalties for offences under Part I of the Act concerning wildlife. The fines in section 21 are as substituted by the Criminal Justice Act 1991, s 17. The "special penalty" which can be imposed for the more serious offences under the 1981 Act is a fine not exceeding level 5 on the standard scale—currently £5,000. Otherwise, the maximum fine varies according to which offence is committed. Where the offender commits an offence involving more than one bird, nest, egg, animal, plant or whatever, the court in setting a fine may treat the offender as having committed a separate offence in respect of each one (s 21(5)).

On conviction the court must order the forfeiture of any bird, nest, egg, animal, plant or thing in respect of which the offence was committed. It also has power to order the forfeiture of any vehicle, animal, weapon or thing used to commit the offence (s 21(6)). This can be a powerful deterrent when it is remembered that a "vehicle" includes an aircraft, hovercraft or boat (s 27(1)).

(d) Attempts and possession of wherewithal

An attempt to commit an offence in Part I of the 1981 Act is itself an offence. So is the possession of anything capable of being used to commit an offence, provided that the possessor has it for the purpose of doing so (s 18).

E. Fish and fisheries

The rare Allis Shad, Burbot, Vendace and Whitefish, along with certain shrimps, sea anemones, Freshwater Pearl Mussel, Lagoon Sandworm and Sturgeon are given the protection of the 1981 Act by being included in Schedule 5. The principal legislation governing salmon, trout, freshwater fish and eel fisheries and their fish is the Salmon and Freshwater Fisheries Act 1975 ("the 1975 Act"). It is a useful measure for conservation, and it is aided and abetted by the Salmon Act 1986. The body of legislation governing commercial sea fishing, which to an extent protects species from over-exploitation, is outside the scope of this book.

1. Salmon and Freshwater Fisheries Act 1975

The Act extends to England and Wales, with a few peripheral provisions affecting Scotland (s 43). It is a comprehensive code, outlined here only so far as it is relevant to conservation.

(a) Meaning of "freshwater fish"

The 1975 Act defines "freshwater fish" to mean "any fish living in freshwater exclusive of salmon and trout and of any kinds of fish which migrate to and from tidal waters and of eels" (s 41(1)).

(b) Unlawful methods and devices

The 1975 Act makes it an offence to use or possess, without the written consent of the National Rivers Authority ("NRA"), certain devices for taking or killing salmon, trout or freshwater fish, namely any firearm within the meaning of the Firearms Act 1968; otter, lath or jack, wire or snare; crossline or setline; spear, gaff, stroke-haul, snatch or other like instrument; or a light. Barbless gaffs and tailers may be used "as auxiliary to angling with rod and line" (s 1). The devices named are no mystery to the poaching fraternity, but the meaning of the more esoteric terms can be found in s 1(3). "Otter" does not mean the animal, but a device for running out lures.

The 1975 Act bans the use of missiles (s 1(1)(c)) and fish roe for fishing (s 2), and has provisions against poisons and polluting matter, explosives, electrical devices and destruction of dams (ss 4, 5), and regulates the use of nets (s 3) without NRA written permission.

(c) Obstructions to the passage of fish

Part II of the 1975 Act contains a series of provisions and offences to secure the passage of migratory fish up and down rivers, and restricts fishing, otherwise than with rod and line, for salmon and migratory trout at places where they are easy pickings above or below obstructions or in mill-races (s 17).

(d) Close seasons and fishing licences

Standard close seasons and close times are laid down in Part III of the 1975 Act for taking (or attempting to take) salmon, trout and freshwater fish, and for the use of eel baskets. Close seasons may be, and are, much varied by byelaws. Part IV of the Act makes it illegal to fish without a fishing licence by rod and line, net or other means for salmon, trout, freshwater fish or eels.

(e) Administration and responsibility

A duty to maintain, improve and develop salmon, trout, freshwater and eel fisheries is imposed on the NRA by section 114 of the Water Resources Act 1991. The NRA has the general responsibility for operating the 1975 Act and for control of fisheries, though the Minister of Agriculture and the Secretary of State also have powers in this respect (Part V of the Water Resources Act 1991). The NRA has Regional Fisheries Advisory Committees. They perform an influential function, and their members are useful contacts in the event of problems arising with regard to fisheries. Their names and addresses can be obtained from regional offices of the NRA.

2. Salmon Act 1986

The Salmon Act 1986 brushes up provisions of the 1975 Act to do with the use of "fixed engines", the introduction of fish into fish farms, penalties, fishing licences and byelaws of sea fisheries committees. It introduced a new offence of handling salmon in suspicious circumstances, but on the whole it has been a disappointment as a weapon for tackling the multi-million pound business of salmon poaching. The idea of a tagging scheme has been rejected, and the promising provision in the

Act to introduce dealer licensing requires the Minister to make an order to effect it, and this has not been done.

3. Other legislation

(a) Disease of fish

A constant threat to our fisheries is disease. So far, the legislation has been equal to the task of seeing off a succession of harmful diseases which have got into fish stocks, though it has not been successful in preventing the importation of them in the first place. The danger of infectious fish diseases spreading has been increased by the burgeoning number of fish farms. One check is in section 30 of the 1975 Act by which it is an offence to introduce fish or spawn of fish into an inland water without the written consent of the NRA.

The Diseases of Fish Acts 1937 and 1983 control the import of live fish and eggs of fish. The Minister of Agriculture can designate infected areas where disease of fish is detected or suspected. In the designated areas the movement of fish or eggs may be prevented or regulated, and directions may be given to fish farmers regarding the removal of dead or dying fish. Fish farmers must report to MAFF any signs of suspected notifiable diseases. The British Trout Association has a Code of Practice for the Production of Rainbow Trout, which is full of sound advice for preventing pollution and the spread of disease.

(b) Unwelcome species

The establishment of non-native fish species can be a threat to the aquatic environment, and for this reason the Minister of Agriculture is given power by the Import of Live Fish (England and Wales) Act 1980 to control or ban the import of species that he considers "might compete with, displace, prey on or harm the habitat of" any fish in England or Wales. An example of ministerial caution can be seen in the wariness of MAFF to allow stocking of Chinese Grass Carp because of their capacity for consuming aquatic weeds.

As we have seen above, the 1981 Act makes it an offence to release into the wild creatures listed in Schedule 9. The schedule includes Large-mouthed Bass, Rock Bass, Bitterling, Pumpkinseed (the many-splendoured Sunfish), Wels and Zander.

F. Endangered species

English law makes its contribution to the conservation of creatures and plants which are endangered species worldwide, by controlling trade in them within the UK jurisdiction. The Endangered Species (Import and Export) Act 1976 (as considerably amended by Sch 10 to the 1981 Act) contains a range of offences and provisions to prohibit or regulate importing, exporting, buying and selling endangered species, alive or dead, parts of them, derivatives from them, or anything made wholly or partly from them. Much of the Act is broadly modelled on the trading provisions in the 1981 Act. Although some trade can be effected under official licences, the permissive powers of the Secretary of State are subject to the advice of "relevant scientific authorities".

The many pages of schedules to the Act make a useful checklist of the endangered species in the world (including, incidentally, the primate delightfully named the Aye-aye, and a crocodile called the Mugger).

Chapter 8

Buildings and historic sites in the countryside

Abbreviations in this chapter:

AMAAA 1979   = *Ancient Monuments and Archaeological Areas Act 1979*

Pl(LB & CA) 1990 = *Planning (Listed Buildings and Conservation Areas) Act 1990*

English Heritage   = *Historic Buildings and Monuments Commission for England*

Cadw   = *Welsh Historic Monuments Commission*

CA   = *Conservation area*

NB: For the meaning of "Secretary of State", see pages 24 and 142–143.

As the Planning Policy Guidance PPG7 reminds us, "the countryside contains a large number of historic buildings and areas" and is "rich in the remains of human activity over thousands of years". Its riches encompass sites, buildings and other structures, ancient or modern, fascinating for their antiquity, or history, or archaeology, or architecture or their associations. They are a joy today. The law gives a fair chance that a good proportion of them will remain a joy for ever—even if some, such as the listed gasholder featured in *Carlisle CC* v *British Gas plc* (1992) 7 PAD 377, are not things of beauty. This chapter points out how, and how far, this heritage is protected and preserved by the designation of conservation areas, the listing of buildings, the scheduling of monuments and other planning tools. There are more than 7,500 conservation areas, 500,000 listed buildings and 21,000 scheduled monuments (White Paper 1990: *This Common Inheritance*). The numbers are continually increasing.

In the consolidation of the planning legislation in 1990, the laws for conservation areas and the listing of buildings were conveniently separated from other planning legislation in the Planning (Listed Buildings and Conservation Areas) Act 1990 ("Pl(LB & CA) 1990"). No sooner was it done than the convenience was significantly undone by the Planning and Compensation Act 1991, Schedule 3 making substantial additions and amendments. Certain procedures and other details are provided for by SI 1990 No 1519. The division of responsibilities following the creation of the Department of National Heritage in April 1992 is noted at the end of the chapter.

A. Conservation areas

Individual buildings and monuments can be given the protection of listing or scheduling. To preserve the character of an area, such as a street, square, terrace, courtyard, close, park or village green, where the buildings, or most of them, do not merit individual listing, conservation area designation can be brought into play. In a conservation area ("CA") the planning authority has special conservation duties, and trees have the added protection described in Chapter 5.

The 7,500 CAs are nearly all urban, or in rural villages. It would appear from the decision of McCullough J in *R* v *Canterbury CC, ex parte Halford* [1992] NPC 21 that a country area without buildings could be lawfully designated as a CA, though he quashed the designation of a field in that case as inappropriate.

Designation of a CA shall be a local land charge (Pl(LB & CA) 1990, s 69(4)).

1. The duties of the planning authority

The duty of designating CAs falls to the local planning authority. Section 69 of the Pl(LB & CA) 1990 requires every local planning authority to determine from time to time the areas of special architectural or archaeological interest the character or appearance of which it is desirable to preserve or enhance. Such areas must be designated as CAs and the designations notified to the Secretary of State and, for English CAs, to the Historic Buildings and Monuments Commission for England ("English Heritage") (s 70(5)). Guidance on criteria for selecting areas for designation is given in DoE Circular 8/87. The park authority can designate CAs in a national park, and the Broads Authority in the Broads.

The planning authority must review past designations from time to time and decide whether to make new designations.

Proposals must be formulated for the preservation and enhancement of CAs, and submitted to a local public meeting. The local authority must have regard to any views expressed. In exercising its powers, a local planning authority is to pay special attention to preserving or enhancing the character or appearance of CAs (s 72).

(a) "Preserving or enhancing"

The question arose in *South Lakeland DC* v *Secretary of State for the Environment* [1992] 2 WLR 204 (HL), whether the duty of "preserving or enhancing" the character or appearance of a CA meant that a development should not be allowed in a CA which, whilst not detracting from its character or appearance, did not positively preserve or enhance

127

it. The whole village of Cartmel, Cumbria, was a CA. The Diocesan Parsonages Board had been refused planning permission to build a new vicarage within the curtilage of an old one in the village, but the Secretary of State allowed the Board's appeal on the ground that the new vicarage would not adversely affect the CA, if properly designed. The House of Lords agreed with the interpretation by Mann LJ in the Court of Appeal that the statutory object "is achieved either by a positive contribution to preservation or by development which leaves character or appearance unharmed, that is to say, preserved". Planning permission was therefore upheld.

2. The power of the Secretary of State

The Secretary of State also has the power to designate CAs (s 69(3)) but only after consultation with the local authority (s 70(3)). He can also disapply designations (s 75(2)). It is believed that these powers have never been exercised, but if they are exercised the local authority must be notified as must, in the case of English CAs, English Heritage.

3. Effect of designation

When a CA is designated, the following consequences arise.

(a) Local authority's duty

The local authority has the duty to preserve or enhance referred to above. A planning permission for development in a CA, given to itself by a planning authority without including in the advertisement of it the time for objection, was quashed by the High Court (*R* v *Lambeth LBC ex parte Sharp* [1987] JPL 440 Court of Appeal).

(b) Deemed planning permission

Limits are placed on developments which would otherwise be deemed to be permitted (a CA is "article 1(5) land" under the General Development Order 1988, SI 1988 No 1813). For example, there are greater restrictions in respect of the alterations that may be made to dwellinghouses, and to constructions in the curtilage of them, without formal planning permission, and the cladding of exteriors needs planning consent.

(c) Planning

Planning authorities are relied on to a large extent to prevent development in CAs which defeats the purpose of designation. To keep them on their toes they are required to publicise applications for planning consents affecting CAs, thereby giving the public an opportunity to make representations (Pl(LB & CA) 1990, s 73).

(d) Demolitions

A "conservation area consent" is needed (as well as planning consent) before a building can be lawfully demolished in a CA. Applications for consent are made to the local planning authority. Applications for consent by the local planning authority are made to the Secretary of State (s 74). The provision does not apply to listed and ecclesiastical buildings, ancient monuments and other structures covered by separate legislation (s 75). Procedures for applying for consent, and for variation or revocation of conditions in a consent, are in SI 1990 No 1519.

(e) Urgent repairs

Powers are given to local authorities to do urgent work to keep unoccupied buildings, or unoccupied parts of buildings, in CAs in repair (s 76). The provision for listed buildings (p 134 below) is applied.

(f) Trees

As explained in Chapter 5, there is special protection for trees in CAs.

(g) Advertising

There are minor differences in the planning rules regarding the display of advertisements.

4. Procedures

A local planning authority designates an area as a CA by passing a resolution to that effect. The designation takes effect from the date of the resolution. It is essential that the boundaries of the CA and the properties included in it are clearly defined. This is done by appending a map to the resolution of sufficient scale accompanied by a schedule of the properties within the CA.

No previous public notice need be given before designation, nor need notice be given to owners and occupiers, either before or after designation, even though their rights are restricted. Later purchasers of properties in the CA will have notice because the CA will be registered as a local land charge. In practice some form of public consultation often takes place. The designation must be advertised in the *London Gazette* and at least one local newspaper—never a satisfactory method of drawing attention to the exercise of bureaucratic powers. Nobody has a right of appeal against a designation, but *R v Canterbury CC, ex parte Halford* [1992] NPC 21 shows that the High Court will quash an improper designation on judicial review.

It might be noted that there is no statutory right for developers or others to obtain a statutory certification, similar to that regarding the listing of buildings (see p 136 below), that an area will not in the near future be designated as a CA.

5. Grants and loans

English Heritage, Cadw (Welsh Historic Monuments Commission) and the Secretary of State may make grants or loans towards any expenditure making "a significant contribution towards preserving or enhancing the character or appearance" of a CA or any part of one (s 77). There is no fixed rate of grant. It will be a percentage of approved expenditure, usually not paid until the work has been completed to the satisfaction of the grantor. The usual rate seems to be 25 per cent. Loans can be made if agreement is reached regarding repayment and interest. If the recipient of a grant disposes of his interest in the land or building, he may be required to repay some or all of the grant (s 78).

B. Listed buildings

Ever since the original great Town and Country Planning Act of 1947 there has been a system of identifying and preserving buildings of special interest. They are placed on lists, and a body of law, now found in the Pl(LB & CA) 1990 (as amended) and in statutory instruments, is applied to them. Buildings may be listed because they are fine buildings, or maybe because they are valuable as examples of certain styles of architecture, or building technique, or an innovation in the use of materials, or because of their place in architectural history. Or they may be listed for other historical reasons, such as their association with persons or events of note. Listing is undertaken by the Secretary of State, but the immediate protection of listed buildings is a task of the local planning authority (and see the note on "Departmental Responsibility" at the end of this chapter).

Once listed, a building may not, without consent, be demolished or altered in a fashion changing its archaeological or historical character. If such works are done, the local authority can issue enforcement notices requiring restoration.

Grants may be made for important repairs, and other provisions found in the Pl(LB & CA) 1990, as amended, apply. The section references in this part of the chapter are to that Act unless otherwise indicated. Practitioners may also need to consult SI 1990 No 1519 for further details.

1. Selection for listing

Criteria have been laid down for choosing buildings for listing, currently found in DoE Circular 8/87. Unfortunately selection has at times been farcical, with little knowledge of the building concerned, other than that it looked old, and done with no consultation with the person most likely to know about it, namely the owner. Broadly the guidelines indicate that buildings built before 1700 are to be listed if they are in anything like the original condition; buildings built between 1700 and 1840 will normally be listed, but not automatically; buildings built between 1840 and 1914 are to be listed only if they are of good quality and have character, but the principal work of the main architects should be preserved.

Not only old buildings are listed. The Circular suggests nine categories of modern buildings to be considered for listing. They include places of worship, of entertainment and of education; commercial premises; blocks of flats; houses; housing estates; public buildings; and places associated with transport, such as railway stations.

2. Spot listing

Any person or body may request the Secretary of State (not the local authority) to list a building. The public are encouraged to do so where it is genuinely believed that a building of interest is threatened by demolition or unsympathetic alteration. Full details should be sent to the Department of the Environment (for English buildings) or Cadw (for Welsh buildings). They will be investigated, and if appropriate the building will be listed. This is known as spot listing.

3. Grading

Listed buildings are graded into three rather clumsy categories, Grade I, Grade II* and Grade II. Grade I buildings are of exceptional interest. Grade II* buildings are of particular importance. Grade II buildings are of special interest justifying preservation. The higher the grade, the greater the chance of obtaining a grant for repairs, and the lesser the chance of obtaining listed building consent to demolish or alter the building.

4. What is included in a listing

When a building is on the list, the listed buildings laws apply to the building and to any object or structure fixed to it, and also to any building within the curtilage of it, even though not fixed to it, provided that it forms part of the associated land and has done so since 1 July 1948. These appendages have caused difficulty and litigation. Guidance from the House of Lords on what structures are included is found in *Debenhams plc* v *Westminster CC* [1987] JPL 344. The Court of Appeal held that a building in Kingley Street, London, was included when a building in Regent Street, different in character, but in the same rateable hereditament, was listed. In the past the two buildings had been linked by a subway and a second-floor footbridge. The House of Lords reversed the decision, saying that the Kingley Street building, not being an accessory of the listed building, was not included in the listing.

In *Watson-Smyth* v *Secretary of State for the Environment and Cherwell DC* (1991) 64 P & CR 156, Sir Frank Layfield QC held that a ha-ha was capable of being an object or structure within the curtilage of a listed building.

5. Listing procedure

By section 1 of the Pl(LB & CA) 1990 the Secretary of State is responsible for compiling the lists, or approving, with or without modification, lists compiled by English Heritage or other expert bodies. The Act requires the Secretary of State to consult English Heritage, and "other appropriate bodies" before listing an English building. In practice the survey work is undertaken by English Heritage inspectors for English buildings and Cadw for Welsh.

There is still no obligation to consult the owner of the building at any stage, although this might prevent some nonsenses such as the listing of a "mediaeval dove-cot" constructed by the current owner's father. In the past inspectors, who have powers of entry (ss 88–88B), tended to be clandestine. They are now encouraged to approach owners.

The Secretary of State must notify every owner and occupier when a building is listed, or taken off the list, or when some other amendment, such as a change of grading, is made. All listings and amendments are sent to the local authorities for the area, and they as well as the Secretary of State must make them available for public inspection. A copy is deposited as a local land charge (s 2).

6. Implications of listing

There is no absolute duty placed on local planning authorities or the Secretary of State to see, in the performance of their functions, that listed buildings are preserved, but they are enjoined to "have special regard to the desirability of preserving the building or its setting or any features of special architectural or historical interest which it possesses", when considering whether to grant planning permission for development affecting a listed building (s 66(1)).

7. Listed building consent

By section 7 listed building consent from the local planning authority is needed for the demolition of a listed building or an alteration changing its character as a building of architectural or historical interest. Repairs may be such an alteration. Where Welsh slates on the roof of a Grade I building were replaced with asbestos tiles, consent was needed, even though part of the roof had previously been repaired with asbestos tiles (*Bath CC* v *Secretary of State for the Environment & Grosvenor Hotel (Bath)* [1983] JPL 737, Woolf J). Painting or repainting will need consent if it alters the character of the building (*Windsor & Maidenhead BC* v *Secretary of State for the Environment* [1988] JPL 410, Mann J).

By section 9, contravention of section 7 is an offence carrying maximum penalties of six months' imprisonment, or a fine of £20,000, or both, on summary conviction, and two years' imprisonment, an unlimited fine, or both, on indictment. In fixing fines the court must have regard to any financial gain to the offender in consequence of doing the unlawful act. It is a defence to show that the works were urgently needed for reasons of safety, health or the preservation of the buildings provided that they were the minimum needed and notice was given as soon as reasonably possible to the local authority (s 9(3)).

Procedures for obtaining and issuing listed building consents are set out in sections 10–17 and SI 1990 No 1519. The Secretary of State must be notified of applications, and he can call them in for his own decision (ss 12–13). Applications must be advertised in a local newspaper by the planning authority and notified to English Heritage in English cases, thereby enabling objections to be made.

Conditions may be attached to a consent. A consent normally lasts for five years, though a different period may be attached to it. Applicants have a right of appeal against the refusal of consents or against conditions in consents (ss 20–22). A consent may subsequently be revoked or modified by the planning authority or the Secretary of State (ss 23–26). Compensation for loss may be claimed in some circumstances where this happens (ss 28–31). If the owner can show that the land is "incapable of beneficial use" by reason of the refusal of a listed building consent, conditions attached to a consent or revocation of consent, he may serve a listed building purchase notice on the local authority. The local authority may be compelled to purchase the building and its associated land if the notice is confirmed by the Secretary of State (s 32).

8. Listed building enforcement notices

The local planning authority may, where work requiring consent has been done without it, serve a notice requiring specified action to be taken, within a given period, to restore the building to its former state or to alleviate the effect of the unauthorised works. Sections 38–46 deal with these notices. Section 38 sets out the procedures.

The occupier or anyone with a legal interest in the building may appeal against the notice to the Secretary of State. It must reach him before the date when the notice comes into effect (s 39). The minimum time for a notice to take effect is 28 days after service (s 38(4)). Appeals can only be made on grounds set out in section 39(1). These 11 grounds include that the building is not of architectural or historical interest; there has been no contravention; the notice is procedurally invalid, or its content inapt; or the work was urgently needed for reasons of safety, health or preservation of the building. It is open to the appellant to contend that listed building consent should be given for the work done.

Enforcement notices are backed up by the criminal and civil law. It is an offence not to comply with a listed building enforcement notice (s 43). The local authority can seek a more direct remedy by applying to the High Court or a county court for an injunction to stop an actual or anticipated demolition or alteration of a listed building (s 44A).

9. Publicity for planning applications

Where a planning application affects the setting of a listed building, the planning authority must bring it to public notice by advertising it in a local paper and displaying a notice at or near the land involved for a minimum of 7 days, making details available for public inspection. English Heritage must be notified if the building is in England. At least 21 days must be given for representations to be made, and any that are made must be taken into account in dealing with the planning application (s 67).

10. Urgent works to preserve listed buildings

As in the case of a building in a conservation area, the local planning authority has the power to undertake urgent works to preserve an unoccupied listed building (s 54), or any unused part of an occupied listed building. The Secretary of State may authorise English Heritage to execute urgent works in England. In Wales, Cadw may undertake them. Seven days' notice must be given to the owner before any works are carried out. The owner may elect to do the repairs himself. If he does, he might obtain a grant for them. If he does not, there is provision enabling the local authority to recover its cost of doing the work. A notice to pay the expenses of the works is served on the owner. He may appeal to the Secretary of State on the grounds that the works were unnecessary, or temporary works were continued for an unreasonably long period, or the amount charged is unreasonable, or recovery of the expenses would cause him hardship (s 55).

11. Compulsory purchase of listed buildings needing repair

A local authority, national park authority, the Broads Authority and the Secretary of State have power to purchase listed buildings compulsorily (s 47). It is obviously a recourse to be resorted to in exceptional circumstances only, where public ownership is considered necessary to keep the building properly maintained. Before compulsory acquisition can take place a repairs notice must, at least two months before compulsory purchase procedures are put in motion, be served on the owner and occupier specifying the works reasonably needed for the preservation of the building. Compulsory acquisition is under the normal procedures of the Acquisition of Land Act 1981, which give the owner an opportunity to object. The owner has the additional right to apply to the magistrates' court for a stay of proceedings, with an appeal against refusal to the Crown Court (Pl(LB & CA) 1990, s 47(4), (5)).

A compulsory purchase order requires confirmation by the Secretary of State. If confirmed, compensation is payable to the owner, assessed under the usual rules for compulsory acquisition, but with the assumption that listed building consent would be granted for works of alteration or extension of the building, or for its demolition for development (s 49).

The acquiring authority can obviate this full cost of acquisition where the building has deliberately been left derelict with the object of attaining its demolition and redevelopment (s 50). In such cases the authority can put a "direction for minimum compensation in the order". If confirmed, the compensation is not then assessed on the assumption in section 49, but on the assumption that only necessary works of repair and maintenance would be allowed.

12. Grants and loans

Local authorities are empowered to contribute to the preservation of buildings of architectural or historic interest (whether or not listed) by making grants and loans towards the cost of their repair and maintenance (s 57). This is a discretionary power. Listing gives no entitlement to a grant. An authority can make it a condition of a grant that access is afforded to the public (s 57(6)). A grant, or part of it, may be recovered from the grantee if he disposes of his interest within three years, or if he contravenes a condition of the grant (s 58). Grants are also available from English Heritage and Cadw for major repairs to historic buildings. They are made to local authorities as well as owners of building. Grants have tended to be limited to Grades I and II* listed buildings.

C. Unlisted buildings

The Pl(LB & CA) 1990 contains provisions for serving building preservation notices on unlisted buildings, and also a provision whereby a developer can obtain a certificate that a building is not going to be listed in the near future. Section references below again are to this Act.

1. Building preservation notices

Local planning authorities are empowered by section 3 to give prompt protection to buildings of special interest, which appear to be under threat of being destroyed or spoiled. They can issue a building preservation notice. The notice will state that the threatened building appears to be one of architectural or historic interest, that the Secretary of State has been asked to list it, and that it is protected by the notice. The effect is that from the date of service on both the owner and occupier, the building, for a period of six months, is counted as a listed building. If the Secretary of State does not list the building within six months, any pending applications for listed building consent, or enforcement procedures, will lapse and the local authority is barred for twelve months from issuing a further building preservation notice on the building. Any criminal liability occurring during the currency of the notice, however, continues after the notice has lapsed. Compensation may be payable for loss or damage occasioned to persons with an interest in the building— e.g. for breach of a building contract. Schedule 2 deals in detail with the consequences of a notice lapsing.

Where protection is considered so urgent that it cannot wait for service of a building protection notice, a notice having immediate effect can be affixed conspicuously on the building under section 4.

2. Certificates of immunity

The listing of buildings has at times frustrated plans in an advanced stage for development, causing hardship, or at least loss of money, to say nothing of hair, blood, sweat and tears. In an attempt to meet this problem, the Act, by section 6, enables applications to be made to the Secretary of State, or to Cadw, for a certificate that a given building will not be listed during the following five years. Applications can be made by any person, provided that planning permission for the demolition or alteration of the building has been applied for, or granted. The application must be copied to the local planning authority. If the certificate is granted, not only will it be an official guarantee that the building will not be listed for five years, but during that period no building preservation notice can be served. Owners and developers should note, however, that the certificate is no guarantee that the building will not be included in a conservation area.

D. Ancient monuments and areas of archaeological importance

1. Ancient monuments

Long before buildings were listed or conservation areas invented, schedules were prepared of ancient monuments singled out for legal protection. It started with the Ancient Monuments Protection Act 1882, protecting 68 sites scheduled in the Act itself. The current legislation is the Ancient Monuments and Archaeological Areas Act 1979 ("AMAAA 1979") as amended by the National Heritage Act 1983 and, to a lesser extent, by later statutes. The official schedule now contains over 21,000 entries and is rising rapidly under English Heritage's Monuments Protection Programme. The section references below are to the AMAAA 1979 as amended.

Whilst listed buildings are in the main inhabited, most scheduled monuments are not habitations. Some are sites of immense antiquity. The majority are remains, ruins and relics. We find in the schedule what is left of old castles, forts, monasteries, early settlements, burial grounds, earthworks, ancient stones with hieroglyphics inscribed on them and the like. We also find monuments in better condition, such as the Tower of London.

(a) *The scheme of the Act*

The AMAAA 1979 has similarities with the Pl(LB & CA) 1990 examined above. To qualify for scheduling, a monument must be a "monument" as defined in the Act. Once a monument is scheduled, certain kinds of works set out in the Act must not be executed to the monument without official consent, and it is a criminal offence to do them without it. There are provisions for urgent works for the preservation of scheduled monuments; compulsory purchase; compensation when the operation of the Act causes loss; and grants for repairing monuments. There are no enforcement provisions like those for listed buildings. Arrangements are made for guardianship and management agreements.

(b) Definitions

The breadth of the schedule of ancient monuments is indicated by some of the definitions.

"Monument" is defined in section 61(7) as—

"(a) any building, structure or work, whether above or below the surface of the land, and any cave or excavation;

(b) any site comprising the remains of such building, structure or work or any cave or excavation; and

(c) any site comprising, or comprising the remains of, any vehicle, vessel, aircraft, or other moveable structure, or part thereof which neither constitutes nor forms part of any work which is a monument within (a) above,

and any machinery attached to a monument shall be regarded as part of the monument if it could not be detached without being dismantled".

A monument includes the site of a monument, and can be a group or any part of a group of monuments (s 61(10)), and the *"site"* of a monument includes so much of the adjoining land as is essential for the monument's support and preservation (s 61(9)). Excluded from the definition are ecclesiastical buildings in use for ecclesiastical purposes, sites comprising objects or remains of no public interest, and sites of wrecks protected by the Protection of Wrecks Act 1973.

"Remains" include any traces or sign of the previous existence of the thing in question (s 61(13)).

"Ancient monument" is any scheduled monument and any other monument which in the opinion of the Secretary of State is of public interest by reason of the historic, architectural, traditional, artistic or archaeological interest attaching to it (s 61(12)).

(c) Duty to schedule ancient monuments

Section 1 requires the Secretary of State to compile and maintain a schedule of monuments. It must contain those scheduled under previous Ancient Monuments Acts. It "may" include any monument which appears to the Secretary of State of national interest, but it must not contain any structure occupied as a dwellinghouse of a person other than an employed caretaker and his family.

The Secretary of State must consult English Heritage before scheduling an English monument. He has power to exclude or amend entries. After scheduling or excluding a monument or amending an entry, the owner, and occupier (if different), and the local authority must be informed and copies of the entry must be sent to them. The up-to-date schedule must be published from time to time. There is no appeal against scheduling. An entry in the schedule is a local land charge (s 1(9)).

(d) Control of works to scheduled monuments

Section 2 sets out works which cannot lawfully be carried out to a scheduled monument without the authority of a "scheduled monument consent" granted by the Secretary of State. These works are—

   (i)   demolishing, destroying or damaging a scheduled monument;
   (ii) removing, repairing, altering or making additions to a scheduled monument, or any part of it;
   (iii) flooding or tipping operations on land in, on or under a scheduled monument.

Blanket consent may be given, after consulting English Heritage, by an order under section 3, to any class or description of work. An order of 1981, SI 1981 No 1302 (amended by SI 1984 No 222), gives consent to six classes of work, including certain agricultural, horticultural and forestry works.

Applications for consent are made to the Secretary of State (not the local authority). The procedure is given in Schedule 1 to AMAAA 1979 (but see also SI 1981 No 1301 for prescribed forms).

If a consent is given, conditions may be attached to it; the consent will remain valid for five years, though there is power to modify or revoke it in the meantime (s 4). Unlike listed building consents, there is no requirement to advertise applications for scheduled monument consent, and only the owner, occupier and the local authority have the right to express a view on the application. Even so, the Secretary of State may hold a public inquiry or offer a hearing. If he does, he must take into account any representations made, and the report of the inspector.

(e) Offences

The AMAAA 1979 creates a number of offences. They are—

   (i)   Executing or causing or permitting any works requiring scheduled monument consent without the authority of such a consent (s 2(1)).
   (ii) Failing to comply with a condition attached to a consent (s 2(7)).

It is a defence to these two offences for the accused to prove that he took all reasonable precautions and exercised all due diligence to avoid or prevent damage to the monument, or, as the case may be, to avoid contravening the condition. It is also a defence to prove that the accused did not know and had no reason to believe that the monument was within the area affected by the works or (as the case may be) was a scheduled monument. A further defence is to prove that the works were urgently necessary in the interests of safety or health and notice in writing of the need for the works was given to the Secretary of State as soon as was reasonably practicable (s 2(7), (8), (9)).

The penalty for these offences, on summary trial or indictment, is a fine. In *R* v *Sims*, The Times, 28 July 1992, the Court of Appeal reduced a fine of £75,000 for an offence under section 2(1) to £15,000 because the damage was not a deliberate flouting of the law, but negligence.

(iii) It is an offence for a person without lawful excuse to destroy or damage a "protected monument", with intent or recklessly, knowing it to be a protected monument (s 28(1)).

"Protected monument" means any scheduled monument and any monument under the ownership or guardianship of the Secretary of State or a local authority (s 28(3)). The penalty on conviction is a fine, or imprisonment up to six months, or both, on summary trial, or on indictment a fine, or up to two years' imprisonment, or both.

(iv) The use of metal detectors has caused concern, and it is now an offence to use a metal detector at the site of a "protected monument" (see above for definition) without the written consent of English Heritage (in England) or Cadw (in Wales) (s 42(1)). The penalty is a fine up to £200.

(v) Even more to the point, it is an offence to remove from the site without written consent any object of archaeological or historical interest, discovered with the use of a metal detector (s 42(3)). The penalty for this offence is a fine up to the statutory maximum (currently £5,000—Criminal Justice Act 1991, s 17) on summary conviction, and unlimited on indictment.

It is a defence to these metal detector offences under section 42 for the accused to prove that he was not using the metal detector to find objects of archaeological or historical interest, or that he had taken all reasonable steps to find out if the site was a protected monument and he believed it was not.

(vi) It is an offence to contravene regulations made to control public access to monuments, or made to safeguard them (s 19(7)).

(f) Compensation

Section 7 provides for compensation to be paid in certain circumstances where the refusal of scheduled monument consent, or conditions attached to a consent, frustrate a development for which planning permission was granted, or deemed, before the scheduling of the monument, provided that the permission remained valid. It is also payable where expenditure has been incurred in lawful works rendered abortive by further works becoming unauthorised (s 9).

Section 27 deals with the assessment of compensation under the Land Compensation Act 1961. Essentially, the compensation is for the depreciation in the value of the land. Practitioners should note that rule 3 in section 5 of the 1961 Act has been amended by the Planning and Compensation Act 1991, Schedule 15 para 1, and that by section 80 and Schedule 18 of the 1991 Act interest is now payable on the compensation from the date of the refusal, or of the grant, subject to conditions, of scheduled monument consent.

(g) Official preservation of monuments

The majority of ancient monuments are privately owned. The Secretary of State, however, does not have to rely on the owners to see to the preservation of nationally important monuments unaided and according to their own devices. The AMAAA 1979 gives the Secretary of State several recourses. He can take an ancient monument, whether or not scheduled, into state ownership by agreement, or by accepting a gift of it with or without associated land (s 11). English Heritage must first be consulted in the case of English monuments. English Heritage and local authorities also have the power of voluntary acquisition. In Wales local authorities and the Secretary of State for Wales can do likewise.

Compulsory acquisition: Powers of compulsory acquisition are given to the Secretary of State. He may exercise it to acquire any ancient monument, whether or not scheduled (s 10), and any land in the vicinity needed for access and the upkeep of the monument (s 15), and rights of way and other easements (s 16). The usual procedures for compulsory acquisition apply under the Acquisition of Land Act 1981.

Guardianship agreements: By section 12, the Secretary of State, English Heritage and local authorities are empowered to enter into agreements whereby they become the guardians of monuments. A guardianship agreement is with the owner. He remains the owner but the responsibility for repair and maintenance is taken on by the body concerned. Compulsory acquisition is a last resort, but voluntary guardianship agreements are common, playing a large part in the preservation of important monuments.

Management agreements: English Heritage also enters into management agreements with farmers for the protection of monuments which could be damaged by agricultural practices. In return for an agreement tailored to protect the monument, but which still allows farming to continue, a tax-free payment is usually made (s 17). The farmer may be required to maintain an undisturbed grass cover over the site; to control erosion by stock; to avoid ploughing the edges of the site; and to control weeds, scrub and rabbits.

Public access: Where a monument is taken into public ownership, or guardianship, the public must be given access to it, though admittance may be restricted or, when needed, suspended (s 19). Admission charges may be made, and facilities may be provided for the public visiting the monument (s 20).

Grants: By section 24, grants may be made towards the cost of preservation, maintenance and management of ancient monuments. English Heritage and Cadw have grant-aid schemes for owners and occupiers of monuments. Owners and occupiers will not usually be paid for routine repairs, but are paid for major repairs, management and archaeological investigations. More details can be found in Chapter 9, p 157 *et seq.*

2. Churches

The position of ecclesiastical buildings used for ecclesiastical purposes is sometimes considered anomalous. Most historic churches are listed, but they are free of much of the restrictive law outlined above. Listed building consent is usually not needed for alterations (or even for demolition where the building is a Church of England redundant church) provided that the building is used for ecclesiastical purposes, other than use as a residence by a minister of religion. Conservation area consent is not normally required either. Further, an ecclesiastical building in use for ecclesiastical purposes is not a 'monument' within the meaning of the AMAAA 1979 and therefore cannot be scheduled. To a large extent, therefore, it is left to planning control to protect such buildings and to the good sense and goodwill of the church authorities.

English Heritage has a special Church Grant Scheme to help with repairs to historic religious buildings of any denomination, Christian or non-Christian. The scheme is under the Historic Buildings and Ancient Monuments Act 1953, s 3A. Further details are given in Chapter 9, p 158.

3. Areas of archaeological importance

The problem of redevelopment of building sites which may be of archaeological importance is tackled by Part II of AMAAA 1979. The difficulty arises where it is not considered right, proper or desirable to prevent the development taking place, but the archaeological implications require investigation before all vestiges are destroyed by the building operations. It has so far been an urban problem in the main, but Part II of the Act could well have application in rural areas, and so it is outlined here.

(a) Designation of areas of archaeological importance

The AMAAA 1979 enables the Secretary of State, a local authority or the Broads Authority to designate areas of archaeological importance (s 33). Procedures are set out in Schedule 2. They differ according to whether it is the Secretary of State or a local authority proposing the designation. There has to be advertisement of the proposal in the usual statutory manner and, if the designation is made, advertisement of the designation. There is no appeal against designation. The designation is a local land charge (s 33(5)). An "investigating authority" may be appointed for a designated area after, in the case of English designations, consultation with English Heritage.

(b) Operations notices

In effect, operations in the designated area involving disturbance of the ground, or flooding, or tipping, can be held up for six months. Any person wishing to carry out such operations must serve an operations notice on the local authority (s 35) unless the operations are exempt operations set out in regulations. The current regulations are set out in SI 1984 No 1286. After an operations notice has been served, the operations cannot be lawfully carried out for six weeks. This gives the investigating authority time to make preliminary investigations and to serve notice that it intends to investigate the site by excavation. The authority can then hold up building operations for four months plus two weeks, but no longer, while it excavates the site.

(c) Offences

By section 35 it is an offence to carry out unexempted operations in a designated area of archaeological importance without serving an operations notice, and it is also an offence to carry out unexempted operations within six weeks after serving an operations notice. Where a site is cleared, the investigating authority must be notified immediately (s 35(7)). If operations are carried out to which the operations notice relates, without giving notice of site clearance, an offence is committed (s 35(8)). The same offences and defences regarding the use of metal detectors at sites of ancient monuments (dealt with at p 139 above) apply to designated areas of archaeological importance (s 42).

Defences to these offences are similar to those under Part I of the Act. It is a defence if the accused proves—

   (i)   he took all reasonable precautions and exercised all due diligence to avoid or prevent disturbance of the ground (s 37(5)); or

  (ii) he did not know and reasonably did not believe the site was in a designated area (s 37(6)(a)); or

 (iii) the operations were urgently necessary in the interests of safety or health, and notice in writing of the operations was given to the Secretary of State as soon as was reasonably practicable (s 37(6)(b)).

4. Departmental responsibility

Before the Department of National Heritage was created in 1992 the ministerial responsibility for the protection of buildings and sites of historical, architectural or archaeological importance fell to one

Department of State in England, namely the Department of the Environment. It is now shared in an odd manner between two departments. Broadly, so far as the duties fall to "the Secretary of State", the Department of National Heritage is responsible for policy, scheduling ancient monuments, listing buildings and designating conservation areas and areas of archaeological importance, whilst the Department of the Environment handles the "case work", administering the controls in particular cases. It is a recipe for consternation, and by divorcing policy from case work, hardly conducive to soundness in either. It will be interesting to see how, and whether, this state of affairs continues.

(a) Wales

Apart from some differences in procedures, the law is the same in England and Wales, but Wales has its own set-up. The Secretary of State for Wales has general responsibility, and Cadw performs executive functions as an arm of the Welsh Office. In England, English Heritage acts as agent for the Department of the Environment and the Department of National Heritage.

"The Secretary of State" in these laws can therefore mean any of three Ministers, according to what function is performed, and whether its subject is in England or Wales.

This chapter does not attempt to cover the law for Scotland, where there is yet another set-up.

Chapter 9

Conservation initiatives for farmers, landowners and communities

Abbreviations in this chapter:

MAFF = *Ministry (or Minister) of Agriculture, Fisheries and Food*
WOAD = *Welsh Office Agriculture Department*

Laws may be passed by the bookful, and official and unofficial conservation bodies formed, but in the end the welfare of the countryside depends on the stewardship of its owners and occupiers. That stewardship exists and has always existed. The character of the countryside that we know and love is mostly man-made. It is sculpted by those who make their living from the land, those who own it and those who live in it. They have created the rural landscape—the harmonious pattern of fields, woodlands, hedgerows, ditches, farm steadings, hamlets, parks, paddocks and dwellings, fine or humble, with grazing livestock and pastoral artefacts enhancing the general effect. They see that the countryside flows with milk and honey instead of becoming the wilderness of thicket and swamp which only extreme environmentalists would have.

The farmers and landowners have borne the responsibility of nurturing the land, and they have been subjected to a degree of scorn for farming exploitation in response to national agricultural policies. During World War II and for three decades after it, farmers were annually called on to increase production, and they met the call. Grant-aid was given for improving "farming efficiency", and for practices which are now seen to be environmentally damaging.

But there has been a somersault. For many years farm incomes, in real terms, have been sliding. The EC demands lower production of staple commodities. Grants are no longer made to encourage efficient farming, but to discourage it. They are dispensed to achieve land uses and farming methods which are unprofitable, to set-aside arable land, to farm for low yields, to plant woodlands and to provide environmental services for the community. The policy benefits the environment, though a danger looms of environmental damage from neglect of the land where danger once came from intensive farming of it.

None cares for the beauty and well-being of the countryside more than the owners and occupiers of it. The somersault in national policies has caused them vicissitudes, but the switch in the direction of grant-aid, and the increased resources of the nature conservancies and the Countryside Commission, give them new opportunities for conservation and the protection of the national heritage in the countryside. Management agreements noted in Chapter 5 and the schemes described in this chapter forge useful links in the legal conservation chain and get folk involved in conservation work.

A. Grant schemes of the Agriculture Departments

The Agriculture Act 1970 enabled capital grants to be made by the Agriculture Departments towards expenditure incurred in carrying on, or establishing, farm businesses. The Agriculture Act 1986, s 22 widened the ambit of agricultural grant-aid by allowing capital grants to be paid towards businesses ancillary to established agricultural businesses, and the Farm Land and Rural Development Act 1988 allows the payment of non-capital grants. The Ministry of Agriculture, Fisheries and Food (MAFF) and the Welsh Office Agriculture Department (WOAD) thereby have flexibility in setting up schemes by making orders, without the need for new primary legislation. Explanatory leaflets and application forms for the various MAFF and WOAD schemes discussed here can be obtained from their local regional offices.

1. Two warnings

(a) Applicants for grants from the Agriculture Departments must beware of starting work too soon, as grants are not retrospective. Wait for the green light from the Department before going ahead, or entering a binding contract for the work to be done. This generally is the rule also with the other grants referred to in this chapter.

(b) Information given in applications for grants should be checked carefully, especially as it is an offence under the Agriculture Act 1970, s 29 for a person to make a false statement knowingly or recklessly for the purpose of obtaining a grant for himself or any other person. In *Lawrence v Ministry of Agriculture, Fisheries and Food*, The Times, 26 February 1992, the Divisional Court cleared up the issue of where and when such an offence is committed for the purposes of determining the jurisdiction of justices.

2. Farm diversification

One of the tactics aimed to reduce farm produce in surplus in the European Community was to introduce government schemes to help farmers diversify into alternative uses of their productive land. The option of entering the Farm Diversification Grant Scheme is no longer open at the time of writing, as grants were halted from 18 January 1993 under the Chancellor's public expenditure plans, and it is not known if, or when, they will be resumed. As mentioned in Chapter 1, p 8, a feature of the grant-aid, as with other MAFF and WOAD grants, was the requirement of "cross compliance" for the protection of the environment.

Farmers can and will continue to diversify without the aid of government schemes. When they do, planning permission will be needed for non-agricultural enterprises, other than forestry, and non-domestic rating will be attracted.

3. Farm and Conservation Grants Schemes

Under the Farm and Conservation Grants Schemes 1989 and 1991, grants are made to farmers and horticulturalists by MAFF and WOAD towards capital expenditure on work which has an environmental value. These are schemes, unlike set-aside, to help farmers achieve efficient farming, whilst conserving the countryside and wildlife. The grants go partly towards productive agricultural works and partly for conservation, and they can be made for farm diversification. The kinds of works that may be grant-aided include capital expenditure on traditional field boundaries (hedges, fences, walls and banks); works to prevent pollution from farm effluents; heather and bracken management; shelter belts; reseeding and regeneration of grassland; supply and installation of energy-saving facilities; repair and reinstatement of traditional farm buildings; and other works.

(a) Eligibility

All established agricultural and horticultural businesses are eligible for grants under the 1989 Scheme. The range of grants is wider under the 1991 scheme, but there are tight eligibility rules allowing grants only through an Improvement Plan for businesses which earn less than an amount known as "reference income" for every 2,200 hours worked. The Improvement Plan is an approved programme of investments to improve the farm and to improve or maintain the income from it. The "reference income" is a fixed figure laid down annually by the Department.

The applicant must either have been farming for at least five years or hold a suitable training certificate. He must spend at least 1,100 hours a year working on the farm business and receive at least 50 per cent of his annual income from it and allied businesses, if any, on the farm. At least 25 per cent of the annual income must be from the purely agricultural part of the business.

Special rules are laid down for dairy, pig and poultry enterprises.

To qualify for grant the work must generally have a life of at least 10 years, or 20 years for pollution control facilities.

(b) The grants

Higher rates of grants are payable in Less Favoured Areas (LFAs) than elsewhere. Grants range from 15 per cent (25 per cent in LFAs) to 40 per cent (50 per cent in LFAs) of eligible expenditure to a ceiling of £40,000. Young farmers (under age 40) can get a 25 per cent increase of grant under Improvement Plan schemes.

4. Set-aside

An indication of the extraordinary pass we have reached in Europe is that farmers in the Community are now being bribed not to farm their land. Since 1988 there have been a number of set-aside schemes in an attempt to reduce surpluses in European intervention stores. All set-aside schemes are voluntary. Farmers enter them by making application. MAFF estimates the amount of land in the UK taken out of production by the end of 1993 to be 1.5m acres. There has been a consequential conservation benefit. A survey in southern and eastern England by the Royal Society for the Protection of Birds disclosed that three times as many wild birds inhabited set-aside fields as arable fields.

(a) Environmental and amenity protection

Land retained in fallow can become an unattractive jungle dominated by harmful weeds. Fortunately, land can be set-aside in a manner to improve habitats in field headlands, to link other habitats such as woods and copses and to encourage diversity of flora and attract bird life. The Departments encourage these methods in their set-aside scheme, and under the "cross compliance" policy impose safeguards designed to ensure proper maintenance of set-aside land and other environmental advantages. Set-aside schemes are voluntary, but there is talk of compulsory set-aside emanating from Europe. Twenty-year set-aside plans are under discussion.

(b) The current scheme

At the time of writing, the EC rules for set-aside have not been fully settled following the reform of the Common Agricultural Policy in 1992, and the scheme for 1992–1993, set out here, is subject to change. A scheme for five-year set-aside under somewhat different rules preceded it. This scheme is closed, but those already in can continue in it. There was also a temporary one-year scheme for 1991–1992. The rules are strict and pernickety, because they are designed firstly to achieve the purpose of reducing arable cropping, and secondly to avoid fraud. The main features are—

- The set-aside land must have been cultivated in the previous year with the intention of producing a harvestable crop, unless it was set-aside under a previous scheme. Permanent grassland, woodland and non-agricultural land is therefore excluded.

- A minimum area of the farmer's arable land must be set-aside under the scheme. This requirement is not straightforward. The minimum takes into account any area for which area payments (referred to below) are claimed, and any land in the five-year scheme. As a guide, the minimum must come to 15 per cent of the sum total of the area on which area payments are claimed and the area set-aside under the scheme.
- The set-aside land must not be used for agricultural production, grazing livestock or any activity involving a return in cash or kind, except that crops for certain non-food products may be grown.
- To avoid the risk of nitrate leaching, the set-aside land must not be left bare over the winter. A green cover must be obtained, either by sowing, or by allowing natural regeneration of the preceding crop or plant cover.
- No fungicides, insecticides or fertilisers (other than lime) may be applied without permission, subject to an exception for manure from the same holding. Permission may be given to use fertiliser to create a lush sward as a feeding area for migratory geese. Herbicides may be used only as spot treatment or with a wick applicator to control weeds, unless, in exceptional cases, permission is given to spray them.
- Certain "environmental features" on or adjacent to the set-aside land must be maintained. They include traditional buildings, stone walls, hedges and ponds.

(c) Grants and area payments

To compensate the farmer for taking productive land out of profitable use, set-aside grants are made annually by MAFF and WOAD, determined in ecus by the EC.

Under the reform of the CAP, support prices for cereals were substantially reduced, but new "area payments" were introduced in two schemes ("main" and "simplified") for land used to grow cereals, oilseeds and proteins. Rules of eligibility are laid down as to crops and the type of land for which the payments may be claimed. They are not given here, but they are mentioned because the main scheme is linked to the set-aside scheme. In the simplified scheme there is no set-aside requirement, but farmers can only claim on a limited area of land.

Area and set-aside payments are liable to tax as income.

(d) Farm tenants

The Departments do not require tenants to obtain the consent of their landlords before entering the set-aside scheme, but they advise them to notify their landlords in writing first. Tenants should beware that they might be in breach of tenancy by setting aside agricultural land, and possibly in breach of the Rules of Good Husbandry, with serious consequences for their security of tenure. This is discussed in Chapter 5, pp 71–72.

5. Extensification

"Extensification" is an uncomely term of art meaning a reduction in the annual production from an area of land, under a scheme by which the farmer is compensated with annual payments. Two pilot schemes for beef and sheep introduced in 1990 will not be extended, but on the recent reform of the CAP member states of the Community are required by the EC Agri-environment Regulation to bring in livestock extensification schemes. None is ready for the UK at the time of writing.

6. Environmentally sensitive areas (ESAs)

The law for ESAs and management agreements in them are described in Chapter 3, pp 38–39. The object is to get voluntary management agreements with the farmers to achieve the environmental objectives of each ESA. The agreements are with MAFF or WOAD for ten years with an opportunity to opt out after five years. They include a schedule of works to be completed by the farmer within two years. Annual payments are made. They are intended to compensate the farmer for reconciling conservation work with modern farming practices. Grants currently vary between £10 and £350 per ha.

B. Farm woodlands

The Forestry Authority runs the Woodland Grant Scheme to encourage the expansion of private forestry. The Agriculture Departments have a separate Farm Woodland Premium Scheme with an allied purpose though different motive, namely to encourage farmers to take land out of agricultural production and plant it as woodland. The schemes are linked in that the farmer needs the approval of the Forestry Authority under the Woodland Grant Scheme for the planting, before he can enter the Farm Woodland Premium Scheme. He then obtains grants under both schemes.

1. Woodland Grant Scheme

The Woodland Grant Scheme is a successor to the Forestry Grant Scheme and the Broadleaved Woodland Scheme. Establishment grants are payable for the creation of new woodlands, and for restocking woodlands after felling or windblow. Management grants are made for the maintenance of established woodlands and forests.

(a) Establishment grants

Grants are calculated by the hectare planted. The rate varies with the area planted, and more is paid for planting broadleaves than conifers. Where planting is on arable land or "improved grassland" a supplement of £600 per ha is paid for broadleaved species and £400 per ha for conifers, and a Community Woodland Supplement of £950 per ha is paid where new woodlands affording public recreation are created near towns and cities.

"Improved grassland" is a sward comprising, singly, or in a mixture, over half of ryegrass, cocksfoot, timothy or white clover outside Less Favoured Areas, or one-third of the same where it is situated within a Less Favoured Area.

Establishment grants are paid in three instalments—70 per cent on completion of planting, 20 per cent after five years and 10 per cent after a further five years. Where natural regeneration is relied on, 50 per cent of the grant will be paid on the completion of approved work to encourage it, 30 per cent when adequate stocking has been carried out and 20 per cent five years later.

(b) Management grants

The management grants are payable for approved operations to maintain and improve conifer woodlands aged 11 to 20 years, and broadleaved woodlands aged 11 to 40 years. Again the rate of grant depends on the hectarage and whether the woodland is conifer or broadleaved, and a special management grant is available for agreed operations to enhance woodlands of special environmental value, provided that they are at least 11 years old. There is also a £100 one-off grant for professional advice if woodlands are eligible for management grants and have not previously had grants from the Forestry Authority.

2. Farm Woodland Premium Scheme

The Farm Woodland Premium Scheme is a successor to the Farm Woodland Scheme, now closed to new applicants, and offers greater incentive to farmers to plant woodlands. It aims to achieve new broadleaved woodlands in particular, in the interest of providing wildlife habitats and improved landscapes, as well as reducing agricultural production. The enabling Act is the Farm Land and Rural Development Act 1988.

The Farm Woodland Premium Scheme applies only to farmland to be planted up with trees and approved for planting grants under the Woodland Grant Scheme. It must be arable land (of at least three years) or, unless it is in a Less Favoured Area, "improved grassland" (defined above). The minimum area eligible is 1 ha per agricultural unit, and not more than 50 per cent of the unit will be accepted for the grant. A landowner will not be eligible if he has recovered the land from a tenant by a notice to quit for the purpose of development, or a notice to quit contested by a counter-notice from the tenant, unless consent was given to the operation of the notice to quit by the Agricultural Land Tribunal (under the Agricultural Holdings Act 1986) on the ground of "greater hardship" to the landlord.

Plantings in existing woodlands, or for coppice, or planting Christmas Trees or Cricket Bat Willow are not eligible for the Farm Woodland Premium Scheme.

The grants will be paid annually for 15 years in the case of woodlands containing more than 50 per cent of the area in broadleaves, and for 10 years otherwise. The rate of grant is to be revised every 5 years. The recipient must, however, continue to run an agricultural business on the unit—otherwise the payments will cease, and payments already made may be recovered with interest. On a change of ownership the new occupiers will be able to receive the payments, provided that they apply to enter the scheme within 12 months and are accepted.

C. Countryside Commission schemes

The Countryside Commission schemes are for England only. Schemes available to landowners and occupiers in Wales are noted below. In 1992 it was announced that initiatives of the Commission for conservation and public enjoyment of the countryside would be backed by £13m over three years. Applications to enter the schemes should be made to the local regional office of the Countryside Commission.

1. Countryside Stewardship

The aim of Countryside Stewardship is to promote the combination of successful commercial farming and land management with policies for conservation and public enjoyment of the countryside. The present scheme is a three-year pilot exercise for what the Countryside Commission calls "seven classic English landscapes and their wildlife habitats". These are not designated landscapes, but will be where the Commission, in its discretion, accepts proposals from persons responsible for the management of the land to enter into agreements designed to achieve its objects. The intention is to make up to 5,000 contracts, covering 60,000 to 90,000 hectares, with landowners, farmers and other land managers. £3.6m was earmarked for the scheme after the budget for the first year was over-subscribed with 1,200 applicants.

(a) Eligible landscapes

The seven kinds of landscape presently open to Countryside Stewardship are chalk and limestone grassland; lowland heath; river valleys and other waterside landscapes; coastland; uplands; historic landscapes; and old meadow pasture (in limited areas only).

(b) Agreements

Selected applicants enter into ten-year agreements negotiated with the Commission under which suitable conservation conditions are imposed and a degree of public access allowed. The Commission makes annual payments throughout the agreement and meets standard costs for capital works. Maximum annual payments per hectare presently range from £65 for the first five years for regeneration of heather on uplands, to £250 for heathland and historic landscape agreements.

Conservation measures required by agreements are manifold and have included repair of drystone walls; regulation of grazing, including the reduction of herds and flocks; reseeding areas with traditional grasses, or coastal vegetation on coastland, in place of arable cultivation; farming without fertilisers or pesticides; and in general the protection or re-creation of habitats and restoring the traditional farming landscape after intensive cultivation in the past.

2. Hedgerow Incentive Scheme

Traditional cutting and laying of hedges is in danger of becoming a lost art, and miles of hedgerows are being lost annually from poor management, neglect or removal. The Commission's Hedgerow Incentive Scheme offers payments under ten-year agreements with farmers, landowners and other land managers to rescue and maintain hedgerows. The Commission co-ordinates its scheme with the MAFF Farm and Conservation Grant Scheme (noted above) and aims to obtain good hedgerow management throughout whole farms. In January 1993 the Commission announced that £4.3m was allocated to the scheme for three years, sufficient to restore 1,500 miles of hedgerows; 463 farmers had already signed agreements for 400 miles of hedgerows.

The scheme is discretionary. The Commission selects from applications hedgerows that are long-established; or of high wildlife value; or in degraded landscapes; or of special amenity value. Operations eligible for payments include laying, coppicing, planting hedgerow trees, protective fencing and pollarding, but not ordinary annual hedge maintenance carried out on farms.

(a) Payments

The payments are phased over the period of the ten-year plan. Payments per metre include laying £2 (plus 50p for hedges over 1.5m wide); gapping-up £1.75; coppicing £1.50 (plus 50p on hedges over 1.5m wide); three-line wire fencing 50p; restoration of earth banks £3; and per tree—pollarding £17.50; planting 65p; tree surgery £40. £100 will be paid for technical advice and preparation of the plan.

3. Landscape conservation grants

The landscape conservation grants of the Countryside Commission are usually administered on its behalf by local authorities. The object is to manage and create features beneficial to the landscape and the public enjoyment of it. Work eligible for grants includes amenity tree planting and the creation of small woods under 0.25 hectares, as well as management of existing features of this kind; and the conservation of ponds, stone walls, hedgerows and green lanes. Except where the features are trees and woodlands, priority is given to work which is part of a conservation plan for the whole of a farm, arranged with expert advice. The grants are normally between 25 and 50 per cent of the cost of each operation.

4. Rural Action

The Countryside Commission has announced a new scheme called Rural Action to provide grants to enable local people to tackle a range of environmental projects. Funding will be available to local groups through support networks in each county, and also for projects on private land, provided that public access is assured. The kind of projects in mind are restoring ponds, planting trees, creating wildlife habitats, curbing traffic flow through villages, drawing up parish maps and "promoting green tourism". Up to 50 per cent of project costs will be met.

5. Heritage landscapes: capital tax relief

The Capital Transfer Tax Act 1984, Part II, Chapter 2, gives conditional inheritance tax exemption to owners of land of outstanding scenic interest managed under undertakings to preserve its character and allow reasonable public access to it. The Countryside Commission and county councils or national park authorities, acting as the Commission's agents, monitor the conditions for tax exemption. To help both sides, the Commission encourages the preparation of a simple management plan, identifying the exempt land and features of special landscape and heritage importance, setting out management policies and arrangements for public access. The Commission will advise on the content and preparation of the plan and agree the final version, to ensure that exemption is granted. The Inland Revenue has issued a helpful guidance publication on the subject, *Capital Taxation and the National Heritage*, available from The Reading Room, Somerset House, London WC2R 1LB.

D. Schemes of the Countryside Council for Wales

As described on p 19 above, the Countryside Council for Wales performs in Wales functions similar to those of the Countryside Commission and

English Nature. The Council has powers under the Environmental Protection Act 1990 to make management agreements with landowners and occupiers, to pay for work to protect habitats, to compensate owners and occupiers for restrictions on land use, and to aid, by grant or loan, activities carried out by individuals and bodies for the conservation of the countryside and providing public access. It has incentive schemes to foster conservation parallel to those applicable in England, though, being a relatively young authority, some schemes are as yet more limited and, at the time of writing, not fully fledged.

1. General conservation grants

A scheme described as "Grants for Various Programmes and Projects" offers grants to individuals and organisations to carry out conservation work. Its main purposes are conservation of the quality and diversity of nature and landscapes in Wales; supporting the Welsh dimension in Great Britain projects; community initiatives; training professional and voluntary staff; public access; and land purchases for the protection and management of sites, species and landscape features.

The Council may meet up to 50 per cent of total costs.

2. Landscape and Nature Conservation Grants Scheme

Owners, occupiers and others may apply to their local authority for grants, administered on behalf of the Countryside Council for Wales, for financial assistance and guidance in nature conservation projects or in managing or enhancing important landscape features.

3. Tir Cymen—Stewardship Scheme

This is a pilot scheme along the lines of Countryside Stewardship in England, but initially it operates only in three districts in Wales, namely Meirionnydd, Dinefwr and Swansea. Ten-year agreements are made with farmers to produce "environmental market goods" on farm holdings in the three districts, for which annual payments will be made. Annual payments are made also for providing public access where there was none previously. Capital payments are to be made for the re-creation or restoration of habitats or landscape features, and for "low profile facilities".

Acceptance into the scheme is in the discretion of the Council. The kind of "goods" that it suggests that it would make payments for include changing grasslands from ryegrass to flower-rich hay meadows; changing drained pastures to grazed wet grasslands; changing improved grassland or bracken to heather moorland; changing derelict boundaries to stock-proof hedges or maintained walls and cloddiau (quarries); creation of small woodlands protected from grazing; and the provision of improved public access.

4. Hedgerow Incentive Scheme

As with the Countryside Commission's scheme (see p 152 above), payments are to be made for the restoration and maintenance of neglected hedgerows.

E. English Nature grants

Chapter 2 mentions sundry nature conservation enterprises of English Nature (Nature Conservancy Council for England). The Environmental Protection Act 1990, s 134 enables English Nature (and the other conservancies) to "give financial assistance by way of grant or loan (or partly in one way and partly in the other) to any person in respect of expenditure incurred or to be incurred by him in doing anything which in their opinion is conducive to nature conservation or fostering the understanding of nature conservation". In particular, grants are made to owners and occupiers of land under the Project Grants Scheme, as well as under management agreements described in Chapter 5. Applications for grants should be made to the regional office of English Nature.

1. Project grants

The grants are mainly given to conservation organisations for specific costs related to practical projects beneficial to nature conservation, such as the purchase or hire of equipment, employment of temporary staff and interpretative facilities for visitors, and may also extend to computerisation, major wildlife appeals, training and publications. Landowners and farmers may also be assisted with projects, especially for conservation work on land notified as Sites of Special Scientific Interest.

The grants are aimed principally at safeguarding land of special importance to wildlife; providing land management for nature conservation; protecting species of plants, animals and birds threatened with extinction nationally; extending the abundance of selected species locally; encouraging people to become involved in nature conservation projects in their local community; and providing public access to land for the enjoyment of wildlife. Payments may therefore be made towards creating nature trails, and erecting hides and interpretative displays for the public, and for works such as scrub control, control of water levels and fencing.

The grants are discretionary. There is no standard rate, but they may be up to 50 per cent of agreed costs. Works below a minimum cost (currently £200) do not qualify. Occupiers must be in a position to guarantee future management of the land for nature conservation in order to qualify for a grant.

2. Wildlife Enhancement Scheme

This started with a trial scheme with owners and occupiers of land in two areas only, the Pevensey Levels SSSI in East Sussex and a group of Culm Grasslands SSSIs in Devon and North Cornwall. Other pilot schemes are being announced. Payments are made to persons responsible for land management in the selected areas, towards the costs of conserving and enhancing the wildlife in the SSSIs, with the purpose of ensuring that England's finest SSSIs are managed for the benefit of wildlife through the personal involvement and skill of the manager of the land, with his knowledge of the land. Payments are also made to meet the costs of special "one-off" work.

3. English Nature grants for groups

Some other projects of English Nature intended for the participation of groups and organisations, and not farmers and landowners as individuals, are mentioned briefly here. Landowners, however, do get involved in these projects and can, through their private trusts, or their positions on local bodies and organisations, take initiatives to further the specific objectives of English Nature.

(a) The Living Churchyard

Grants may be made, up to 50 per cent of approved costs, for the purchase of equipment and materials, and training and planning for people managing, or intending to manage their churchyard for nature conservation. The maximum grant is currently £500.

(b) Volunteer Action grants

These are offered to County Trusts and other bodies with charitable status to reimburse the travelling expenses of volunteers undertaking work on nature reserves or other work to safeguard species, such as wardening, or installing bat grilles and bird boxes, or organising development of the organisation. The intention is to help smaller organisations put more volunteers in the field. Second-class rail, bus and ferry fares to and from sites are reimbursed, or a car mileage allowance paid, subject to a minimum of £100 a year and a maximum of £1,000 a year for the voluntary body concerned.

(c) Staff-post grants

These grants are for voluntary bodies to set up key full-time or part-time posts so that they may be more effective in nature conservation work. The payments are made towards the employee's salary and the employer's NI contribution and travel expenses for up to three years. Up to 50 per cent of approved costs are paid to a maximum per organisation of £1,000 a year.

(d) Schools grant scheme

Grants are awarded to schools to create a nature area within the school grounds, to give opportunities for learning and direct experience for pupils. The maximum grant is currently £500.

(e) Community Action for Wildlife

It should be noted that this is not a countryside scheme. It aims to promote community involvement in nature conservation projects in towns and cities.

F. Grants for ancient monuments and historic buildings

The laws for the protection of ancient monuments, historic buildings and sites of archaeological importance are described in Chapter 8 where it will be seen that "ancient monument" has a wide definition to cover sites of many kinds. Grants towards their maintenance may be made to owners and occupiers, as well as some public and private bodies, by English Heritage (Historic Buildings and Monuments Commission for England) and Cadw (Welsh Historic Monuments Commission). MAFF and WOAD also can make grants to owners and occupiers of agricultural land and buildings. It is believed that the majority of ancient monument sites are probably not recorded, and English Heritage and Cadw encourage the discovery of unrecorded sites.

1. Management agreements

In many cases sites can be damaged by ordinary farming operations. Chapter 8 refers to management agreements with owners to protect ancient monuments, for which annual tax-free payments are made on a scale agreed with the Country Landowners' Association and the National Farmers' Union based on the dimensions of the sites. The payments are not sufficient to make the agreements profitable, but are intended to see that farmers suffer no loss by protecting the sites. The agreements can include payment of capital costs, and the cost of providing interpretative information and facilities.

2. Ancient monument grants

English Heritage and Cadw will, in their discretion, make grants for major repairs and management of ancient monuments, but not for routine maintenance. Monuments do not have to be scheduled to qualify for grants. Works eligible for grant include major stabilisation and consolidation of structures; repairs to the fabric; repointing masonry;

and repairing earthworks after erosion. All works should be done in consultation with the grantors and under expert guidance. The standard rate of grant is 40 to 50 per cent of approved costs.

(a) Survey grants for presentation purposes

English Heritage makes grants for surveying the evidence of ancient monuments and presenting it to the public. It publishes a guidance booklet setting out the investigations required and what it expects to have presented.

3. Historic buildings grants

English Heritage and Cadw give grants for repairs to historic buildings, provided they are of outstanding national interest. The vast majority will be Grade I and Grade II* listed buildings, but not all buildings of outstanding interest are so graded, and some may not be listed at all. Grants will only be made if the repairs are major (minimum cost £10,000) and beyond the means of the owner. The standard grant is 40 per cent of approved costs.

Grants may also be obtained from the local authority under the Local Authority (Historic Buildings) Act 1962, and MAFF can give grants for repairing traditional farm buildings.

(a) Religious buildings

English Heritage has a special scheme for making grants for repairs to historic religious buildings (not necessarily churches, or Christian) still in use for public worship. Before giving a grant it must be satisfied that the building is of outstanding merit, the repairs are urgent and major, and beyond the means of the congregation. If made, grants will be subject to conditions that an architect is employed; the building will be regularly maintained; all future alterations and additions will be approved by English Heritage; and reasonable public access is allowed. No standard rate of grant is laid down.

G. Rural Development Commission grants

The countryside will not be conserved unless people live and work in it. The importance of a healthy rural economy for the survival of villages and the care of the land cannot be overemphasised. The Rural Development Commission is therefore mentioned here. The Commission does not directly aid conservation work, but it promotes the viability of rural businesses, encouraging employment in the countryside, the utilisation of redundant buildings and the provision of housing in villages and small towns.

1. ACCORD

The Assistance for Co-ordinated Rural Development Scheme (ACCORD) is for companies, individuals and charitable trusts, by which advice and financial assistance is given to the private sector for business enterprises bringing employment and economic benefit to rural areas. For the most part payments are pump-priming loans, payable where other sources of finance have been fully utilised but help from the Commission is still needed for the business project to go ahead. The amount and terms of finance depend upon the circumstances of each case.

2. Redundant buildings grants

These grants are to assist with converting redundant buildings in the countryside for business enterprises creating employment other than in agriculture. The grants are available in Rural Development Areas for owners intending to lease the premises to small businesses. Grants are normally 25 per cent of authorised costs, subject to a maximum, currently £50,000.

H. Miscellaneous sources of grants

This chapter has indicated grant-aid available for conservation enterprises from statutory bodies. Many a good enterprise does not obtain an official grant, either because it does not qualify, or there is not enough money in the pot. The numerous non-statutory schemes of trusts and other organisations aiding landowners, occupiers and groups with worthwhile local projects for the good of the community, should not be overlooked. They can be found in directories, such as *The Green Index* and *Who's Who in the Environment*, or directories of charitable trusts.

Index

171

Notes

...provides the most efficient means of keeping pace with developments in environmental and public health.

Knight's Environmental and Public Health Acts specifically reflects the needs of public health practitioners. It contains all the modern environmental and public health Acts of the 1990's and comes complete with a regular updating service to ensure that the information is always accurate and up-to-date.

Designed for maximum efficiency

This service is specifically designed to save you valuable time and effort. Finding the information you require is made easy with the inclusion of tables which list all the Acts in alphabetical and numerical order, whilst informative headings, a detailed contents list and exhaustive main index will lead you straight to the point in question.

Knight's Environmental and Public Health Acts is available on a subscription basis with approximately 4 updating supplements per year. This year the price of a subscription plus updating service is £250.

Value for money

As with all Charles Knight publications, you can be sure of value for money. The renewal cost will be kept to an absolute minimum, whilst at all times retaining the standards of quality and excellence you expect from Charles Knight Publishing.

Full refund guarantee

You can order Knight's Environmental and Public Health Acts on 21 days' approval, giving you the perfect opportunity to discover in your own working environment just how useful it really is. If you choose not to keep it, simply return it to us in saleable condition and we will refund your payment or cancel your invoice without question.

How to order

To order your copy of this essential work, simply complete and return the order form below to the Customer Services Department, Charles Knight Publishing Company, Tolley House, 2 Addiscombe Road, Croydon, Surrey CR9 5AF or telephone our order-line on 081-686 0115.

ORDER FORM

Charles Knight Publishing Co, FREEPOST, Tolley House, 2 Addiscombe Road, Croydon, CR9 5WZ England

	Price £	No. of copies	Amount £
Knight's Environmental and Public Health Acts	£250		
		Total	

Cheque enclosed for £ _____

Please make cheques payable to: Tolley Publishing Company Ltd

VISA

Please debit Tolley/Access/Visa* account number

Expiry Date (M/Y) _____

Signature _____

Surname* _____ Initials _____ Title (Mr, Mrs, Miss, Ms)

Qualifications _____ Job title _____

Full name of Firm (if applicable) _____

Address* _____

Postcode _____ Telephone _____

*If paying by credit card, please enter name and address of cardholder.
Registered No 729731 England   VAT Registered No 243 3583 67

Notes